Animators Unearthed

Animators Unearthed

A Guide to the Best of Contemporary Animation

CHRIS ROBINSON

continuum

2010

The Continuum International Publishing Group Inc
80 Maiden Lane, New York, NY 10038

The Continuum International Publishing Group Ltd
The Tower Building, 11 York Road, London SE1 7NX

www.continuumbooks.com

Adobe Flash® and Maya® are registered trademarks. The term 'Flash animation'
refers to animation created using Adobe Flash®.

Library of Congress Cataloging-in-Publication Data
Robinson, Chris, 1967-
Animators Unearthed : A Guide to the Best of Contemporary Animation / by
Chris Robinson.
    p. cm.
ISBN-13: 978-0-8264-2956-8 (pbk. : alk. paper)
ISBN-10: 0-8264-2956-4 (pbk. : alk. paper) 1. Animated films—History and
criticism. 2. Animators. I. Title.

NC1765.R619 2010
791.43'340922—dc22   2009053738

ISBN: 978-0-8264-2956-8

Typeset by Pindar NZ, Auckland, New Zealand
Printed and bound in the United States of America

For Mait Laas and Andrea Stokes, whose soul mates left the earth far too soon.

Contents

Illustrations

Introduction

The Struggles of Independent Animation

I'd like to say that the phrase "animation isn't just for kids and acne-scarred teens" is a cliché nowadays, but sadly, it isn't and I'm not entirely confident that it ever will be.

Like animation, comics have long suffered from the same derogatory label, but in the last few decades have emerged as a more recognizable and popular art form for adults. Given the number of adaptations of adult comics/graphic novels that have been made during the last decade (for example, *American Splendour, Ghost World, Watchmen*), the film industry has certainly come to this understanding. Even the literary world has accepted comics (with the fancy name "graphic novels") and many bookstores have even created graphic novel sections. That's quite an achievement for a medium (yes, it's a medium not a genre) that was previously always viewed as kid fodder.

Although independent animation has made major strides in recent years (the recent success of independent/adult animation features like *Persepolis* and *Waltz with Bashir* are prime examples), the belief is that animation is still hampered by the "cartoon" and "entertainment" labels.

Part of the problem is visibility — or rather, lack thereof. In the late 1950s, there were already a number of animators making "art" or "personal" animation, but before I give you a little historical background, perhaps we should go off track a second to explain just what the heck independent- or personal- or art animation is and isn't.

Mainstream animations (often called "cartoons") are usually made for a market place. Their content and style (the overall look) are researched and tailored towards a gender or age group. They're often genre-based, story/character driven and made as episodes with recurring characters. In fact, the success of these works relies heavily on the viewer connecting with the characters — *The Simpsons* is a prime example of this. Even feature animation films are made with the possibility of sequels (for example, *Toy Story*). These works are made by studios and created by many artists working under the supervision of a committee of producers and executives.

Independent-, art- or personal animation avoids genres and are generally written, animated, directed and designed by a single artist. These films are usually self-contained and often use techniques rarely seen in mainstream animation (for example, cameraless animation — which can involve scratching or painting on film, object animation, paint-on-glass, pixilation — and speeding up or manipulating live-action footage). These films are usually funded, owned and distributed entirely by the animator.

Personally, I don't like borders, so let's just consider the above as rough guidelines set in erasable ink. There's a danger when we establish firm definitions. There are some animation purists who refuse to accept computer as animation, and still more brush off mixed-media works that combine live-action and animation (oddly enough, these same snots are the first to hail Norman McLaren as the god of art animation even though he frequently fused live-action and animation).

Also, let's be clear that just because a film is independent, it doesn't mean it's good, just as mainstream animations are not always bad. There are, for example, many animated music videos and TV commercials that rival any work of art, and some people would also hail a TV series like *The Simpsons* as a work of art in itself.

There's often overlap between these two approaches. If we consider independent animation to be "auteur" driven (that is, every part of the work is made by a single author), what do we do with so-called mainstream animation made by auteurs? Betty Boop (The Fleischer brothers), *Fritz the Cat* (Ralph Bakshi), *Ren and Stimpy* (John Kricfalusi), and the classic Looney Tunes shorts (made by a team of artists working under the instructions of a studio producer, yet each short bears the distinctive mark of its own director) are just a few examples of this overlap.

On the independent side, Nick Park (the Wallace and Gromit films), Bill Plympton, PES and Adam Benjamin Elliot (*Harvie Krumpet*) straddle the border between art and entertainment. Each of these examples (in Park's case, he has already crossed over into the mainstream arena) works in a recognizable style and tone, often uses recurring characters and ultimately has an eye towards mainstream success — not that there's anything wrong with that.

In fact, as you'll discover when reading the 20 animator profiles in this book, the line between independent and mainstream, or art and entertainment, is very blurry.

Brief History of Independent Animation

Independent animation dates back to the beginnings of animation. Animation pioneers like J. Stuart Blackton (*Humorous Phases of Funny Faces*, 1906), Emile Cohl (*Phantasmagorie*, 1908), Winsor McCay (*Gertie the Dinosaur*, 1914), Wladyslaw Starewicz (*The Cameraman's Revenge*, 1919, made using real dead insects) and Lotte Reiniger (made her first silhouette film in 1918) were independent, experimental animators. Other early independent animators were Len Lye (whose direct-on-film animations would influence Norman McLaren), Hans Richter, and Oskar Fischinger.

For many, Norman McLaren is considered the Walt Disney of experimental/independent animation. Even though he died over 20 years ago, his films, including *Neighbours*, *Begone Dull Care* and *A Chairy Tale*, continue to influence animation artists around the world.

It's also interesting to note that until the birth of television in the 1950s, animation — even though it was gag orientated — was actually made primarily for adults. Recurring popular characters like Betty Boop, Koko the Clown, Bugs Bunny, Daffy Duck, and Felix the Cat were all made with an eye on an adult audience.

By the 1950s there were independent animators around the world; however, there was a problem. With television veering towards episodic formats, cinemas showing fewer animation shorts (even then, they showed popular studio shorts like Warner Bros.) and film festivals marginalizing or ignoring animation, there were very few places for animators to have their work shown.

In 1960, two events took place that changed the course of independent animation: Annecy, France, hosted the world's first international animation festival (the Annecy International Animated Film Festival), and during the festival, the International Animated Film Association (ASIFA), consisting of animators around the world, was born. ASIFA's aim was to promote and preserve the art of animation.

One of ASIFA's important initiatives was the push and support for more animation festivals. By the mid-1970s, ASIFA was sanctioning Annecy, Zagreb (Croatia) and Ottawa (Canada). Hiroshima would join the group in the mid-1980s. These four festivals — which are all still in existence — are considered the "granddaddies" of the animation festival circuit.

Not only did animation festivals put an emphasis on experimental/independent animation, but they also served as a meeting point for animators. This was especially important during the Cold War period, when travel outside the Iron Curtain was severely limited.

Perhaps the most important impact that ASIFA and animation festivals (and even the National Film Board of Canada which, because of McLaren, attracted animators from around the world) had was that they encouraged the emergence of a new generation of independent animators. In the 1970s in particular, a wave of young animators emerged: George Griffin, David Ehrlich, Ryan Larkin, Pierre Hébert, Suzan Pitt, Priit Pärn (Estonia), Bob Godfrey, Bruno Bozzetto, Renzo Kinoshita, Yuri Norstein (whose 1979 film *Tale of Tales* is routinely hailed as the greatest animation film ever made) and others.

By the late 1990s, independent animation had grown so

much that festivals — which had traditionally been biennial — became annual events. As an example of the growth, the Ottawa International Animation Festival received approximately 750 film submissions in 1992 (these films were made over a two-year period) and by 2008, the now annual festival received over 2,100 submissions.

The growth of the animation industry in the late 1990s played a role in the increase in animation schools and studios and animators. Technology, though, was the biggest motivator: animators who once took anywhere from three to five to ten years to make a film could now turn them around in a year. The rise of the internet also gave animators another means of getting their film to an audience, via YouTube or their own websites.

The days of having to decide whether you were going down the mainstream road or the art road also disappeared, and technology enabled many animators to start up their own studios. Today, smaller, boutique studios exist around the world; these studios tend to balance commercial and independent work, using profits from commissioned jobs to pay for their short films. Some animators, such as Bill Plympton and Nina Paley, have even made their own animation features.

It should be added that independent animation has had a major impact on mainstream animation. While the content is still primarily tepid and conservative, mainstream animation has exploded visually, incorporating many new styles and techniques (often borrowed by the independent world).

What a fantastic story, isn't it? What's not to like? Well, a few things actually. First, visibility is still a problem. While graphic novels have been accepted in the mainstream book world, independent animation still fights for an audience. Television (at least in North America) doesn't have room for short films, and cinemas gave up on short films long ago. Certainly, artists are reaching new audiences through the internet, DVDs, and mobile technology, but 50 years since Annecy hosted international animators, festivals remain the primary exhibition place.

Second, in the comic world, there are a number of magazines that profile the artists and offer critical discussion about their work — this is something seriously lacking in animation. Most of the books about animation focus solely on the history of American animation; you can find endless books with some new perspective on Disney, Pixar, and Bugs Bunny's love of cross-dressing, but the few magazines that exist are little more than press releases for the industry. There are some online websites (awn.com) and blogs (cartoonbrew.com) that offer occasional pieces about independent animators, but for the most part these artists are ignored. When they are acknowledged, it's usually without criticism. How does an art form grow without some hard-hitting feedback?

Another predicament facing both mainstream and independent animators is a general lack of awareness of the artists behind the films. For most people, animation is defined by characters (Mickey Mouse, the Powerpuff Girls, Bart Simpson) or by studios (Pixar, DreamWorks, Disney); however, if you asked these same people who John Lasseter (Pixar), Mike Judge (*King of the Hill*) and Stephen Hillenburg (*SpongeBob SquarePants*) are, they'd likely have no answer.

Animation, one of the most intimate of art forms, remains the most anonymous.

Which leads us to this book. Now, you won't find much hard-hitting criticism in these pages. My primary aim is to introduce you to a selection of international independent animators so that you can learn about who they are, what they do and why they do it.

The choice of animators profiled in the book is highly subjective. Having written an earlier book of animator profiles (*Unsung Heroes of Animation*), I avoided repeats, and I also selected artists that I personally like and some whose work straddles that border between mainstream and independent.

It's my hope that these introductions will encourage you to go out and see more work from these and other fine independent animators.

Figure 1.1   Skip Battaglia

Figure 1.2   *Second Nature*

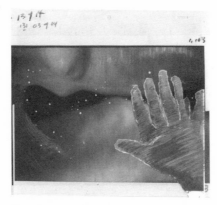

Figure 1.3   *Restlessness*

CHAPTER 1

Skip Battaglia

Skip Man Motion

From his name to life and films, everything about Rochester animator Skip Battaglia speaks movement; Battaglia, an avid hiker and runner, is the perennial traveler, always moving, searching, finding and feeling. His films reflect this hunger for movement and new perspectives. In Battaglia's world, to stand still is to stagnate and to die. To move is to be eternally in motion, mentally, spiritually and physically. When we move, we learn to see differently and become more in sync with our environment.

Battaglia's first meaningful encounter with animation came while he was studying literature in college. "There was a teacher, he was in the English department but he was teaching a film course and he had a short film he was projecting on the wall of his office in 16 mm. Bruce Baillie's *Castro Street* — an experimental film — and I looked at that and came into it in the middle and said, 'What is that?' I said, 'Play that again.' I looked at that and it just had Bruce Baillie's name at the bottom and I thought, 'I didn't know you could make a film by yourself.' You know, I thought you needed accountants and a factory system to make a film. I thought it was a very beautiful, different sort of film."

Born in Buffalo, New York, Battaglia's dad was part-owner of a drive-in movie theater. "I used to show up in my pyjamas, you know, and make it through the cartoons and probably fall asleep in the back seat. And so there was always that experience of, you know, movies were something. My mother would sell the tickets and make the popcorn and my father would run the projector and I would fall asleep."

After studying English literature at Boston College, Battaglia worked a variety of jobs, including editing interviews for a German television show (despite not speaking German), working in a steel plant and teaching at a high school.

In 1975, Battaglia came to Rochester, New York, through a grant he received to set up a film equipment co-op to serve upstate. "I travelled around to different counties teaching community groups how to use film equipment in anticipation of what was going to happen with cable, where, you know, there would be community channels and people would be running around with video cameras and you would be able to get everything on the air."

Battaglia, like so many independent animators, stumbled into animation by chance. While undertaking his master's degree at Syracuse University (SU), he found an animation camera in a back room of the school. "It was a television facility, but the Oxberry [animation camera] was no longer much used for TV graphics. An adjunct teacher had an animated TV graphics course. I offered to become his teaching assistant. After graduation, the teacher let me have a key to the room if I would shoot only Tuesday nights (the evening when he taught). I shot maybe only every 2–3 weeks. I would finish a day's work in Rochester (I had begun to teach part time), pack up the car with materials and drawings, drive the 76 miles to SU, load the camera, shoot till 1 or 2 a.m., unload, drive back to Rochester — getting breakfast along the way — get home at 4 a.m. or 5, appear at part-time work Wednesday at noon. That's how I started with animation. It was very exciting."

Animation attracted Battaglia because of its poetic possibilities. "I had a view of film which was poetic, that you could make a film like you could write a poem or like a writer would make a book. The joy of being able to make something, like a poet, where you're responsible for every image, I only started doing that after I turned 30. I lost a job. I said, 'Well I've got time, I don't have money. I'll draw a film.'"

And that film was *Boccioni's Bike* (1981), an astonishing debut about a bike ride. Inspired by futurist art, Battaglia explores the rhythms of the bike ride from various perspectives. The film begins with a segment of a bicyclist beginning his ride, and then, as he moves and gets more into the flow of his motion, the images break apart, becoming more abstract. Anyone who creates or exercises knows that feeling of getting in the zone, of being so in tune with the motion of your body and surroundings that you lose yourself. Everything momentarily becomes one.

Boccioni's Bike took Battaglia three years to make, "'cause I threw out a year and a half of stuff. I didn't know where it was going and I was reading some futurist materials about the films that still are around. There are only two of the futurist films that are still in collections. And they would take their films and shoot 'em black and white and they would dye them blue. So the films would be black and blue and when asked why they did that, they said because they wanted the film to indicate a state of mind. I said, 'Wow, this is great. This is what I'm drawing. I've channelled futurism.'"

Initially, the images were rotoscoped, but as Battaglia became more confident in his drawing, he stopped rotoscoping altogether. "I picked out a very simple movement, a rotational movement, and once I learned that I stopped rotoscoping. That's why I first threw out the first year and a half of drawings and only kept a couple of them. Partly because it was so obviously rotoscoped and I had begun to learn the movement. The other reason was that I didn't know about pigments and uh, materials to work with and so I was using crayons, which was very flat on the surface of the paper and didn't photograph well. So as I started experimenting with how things photographed I realized I couldn't do work with crayons. I had to use pencils and ink. It would take into the paper. 'Cause I wanted the surface of the paper."

To get the chaotic sound of clinking objects and to create the film's rhythm, Battaglia invited some neighbors over, gave them various tools and got them drunk. "I had bought an 1867 house for $18,000. I was living in it and I was redoing the electricity and everything in the house, so I had all these tools around in the garage. It was like this and we drank a lot of red wine and went in there and we started just pounding tools around. And then I took it on audio tape and I edited it and saw how it went with the film and that gave me a sound track that I could continue drawing on and once I had the audio track down and had it planned out what I was going to do kind of rhythmically and acoustically, then the rest of the drawing on the film took ten months with everything else I did."

For a guy who had not only never made an animation film before, but had never really even drawn, *Boccioni's Bike* is a revelation, a poetic masterpiece that reveals animation's ability to take the viewer on an abstract journey through the subconscious to give voice to the daily unseen of our lives.

While he was making *Boccioni's Bike*, Battaglia started work on a very different film, *Parataxis* (1980). "A Xerox copier was available at the George Eastman House, available for artists to use. I always wanted to make a film with a Xerox machine."

Using a mixture of live-action footage and photocopies, Battaglia shows us a seemingly straightforward image of a man observing a beautiful woman in a fabric shop. As he watches her roam about the shop, we hear a man's voice (we presume it is the same man) talk about the woman, his memory, and why he doesn't approach her. She leaves the store, the two never making contact. The scenario is repeated a second and third time only sound and image have been re-arranged.

The idea for the film's concept came from a variety of sources including poet Joseph Brodsky and Orson Welles's film *Citizen Kane*. "I was teaching *Citizen Kane*. I was teaching a film history course every year and I realized that I was going to have to teach *Citizen Kane* every year of my stupid life. And the character Bernstein says, 'Well, memory's a funny thing.' And so I took the quote from him, about the woman that he saw and hardly a week passes he doesn't remember her, about a woman he saw forty years ago. And then a line from Brodsky's autobiography, 'Am I the story I tell myself?'"

Battaglia then tossed in some other lines, grabbed a notebook, and wrote them down. "Then I took the lines and I wrote them on index cards and then I shuffled them. I was going to call the film 'Shuffle' and maybe I should have. Um, and I did eight shuffles and read it into a microphone and shuffled them again and I took the best four sequences that seemed to tell a story. Later, I arranged the imagery with the soundtrack and realized I only needed three passes and not four. 'Cause I wanted the film to end when people say, 'Oh, we got this figured out.'"

While *Parataxis* couldn't be more visually different from *Boccioni's Bike*, the concept continues Battaglia's fascination with making the invisible visible and giving voice to the unseen everyday workings inside us. As Paul Auster wrote in *The Invention of Solitude*, "memory is the second time an event happened." It's the first time we are telling it from our perspective. Each time we remember an event, something changes, however minute.

How the Frog's Eye Sees (1984) finds Battaglia again dealing with movement and perspective, this time through the eyes of a frog. The viewer is dumped into a pond. We pass through weeds, flies buzz around us until a red tongue lashes out, and there is silence. There are long moments of waiting and sitting as the gentle wind caresses the weeds. Finally, we're immersed in the dark blue of the water. Snippets of a fish appear. There is a flash of red. Then there is nothing.

Frog's Eye sees (pun intended) Battaglia combining elements of cartoons, nature films and abstract imagery (the images of the flies buzzing and almost exploding on the screen transforms into a non-figurative dance of sound and motion) to create, essentially, an almost existentialist film. There is life, then there's nothing.

During this time, Battaglia started his career at the Rochester Institute of Technology (RIT), where he remains today. He'd been teaching film history at St. John Fisher College when he was approached by filmmaker Howard Lester. Lester was in charge of a newly formed film program at RIT and he asked Battaglia to join him.

Many artists admit that there are times when the students actually teach the teachers, by bringing in fresh perspectives about art and technology. That's not quite the case with Battaglia. "Well, with computers, I'm not intuitive about a computer and for this generation, they're much more intuitive about it, so I pick up tricks about technique, but that's not really my interest. I've learned a lot about my students, but not about animation. I wish that they would teach me more."

Like his films, Battaglia's life is about movement. When he's not running, he's hiking across the US. Battaglia began hiking in 1964, and on his most recent hike, in 2007, Battaglia spent 222 days hiking across the US landscape. "When you're running or hiking, you feel you're seeing more somehow because it's the fascination of the landscape propelled past you as you're engaging it."

Geologic Time (1989) is a direct result of Battaglia's hiking experience. A dazzling landscape of clouds, mountains and land rushes by. It's an overwhelming experience, and the images leave as quickly as they enter; there's little time to savour them before they're gone. Suddenly, a man and woman appear, trees fall and buildings explode on the landscape: in an instant, the landscape, the sounds of nature are gone. "That's from hiking. That's from getting stoned and sitting on top of mountains and looking at landscape. Sometimes I swear I could see the curvature of the earth. I started to paint then and I was curious about painting landscape and I wanted a film that was rather painterly."

The theme of man and industry destroying nature is not a particularly new one, but Battaglia does a decent job of avoiding clichés. The ending is sudden, yet from a hiking experience it seems to make sense. For days, weeks, months, there is nothing but trees, grass, clouds, mountains, rivers. Then, in an instant, it's gone, replaced by skyscrapers, gas stations and hotels.

In *Restlessness* (1994), Battaglia delves inside himself for inspiration. Photocopied images of a sleeping naked man race on the screen. The man is still but anxious. Various images appear, seemingly from inside the man: a runner, houses, collapsing houses, a woman, colliding bodies, maps and, most notably, snakes. This diaristic film takes us inside the mind of an artist so that we (and he) can see what imagery is rampant within his subconscious.

"I carried in my dreams, so I kept a dream journal. Also, I was camping out in the desert in Nevada. And it was a public camp area, cause there was water there and they had a concrete block privy and, with poured concrete floor and I'd walk in and there would be a painted snake on the concrete floor. And that's just to tell people to watch out, there might be snakes in here, come in, out of the heat. And I knew that painted snake was there every time. And every time I walked in there, something inside of me jumped. Something just jumped and I said, 'Geez I'm afraid of snakes. What is this?' So, I use the idea of the snake and the whole thing is designed to maintain the imagery of the snake. It's like the roots to tie everything together."

Snakes and frogs aren't the only creatures that have inspired Battaglia's work. In the lighthearted film *Taki Dom* (1997) — a collaboration with Julie Ann Jergens and Dan Pejril — chickens take the stage. Made as a music video for vocal trio called F'loom, *Taki Dom* features chickens — in whole and in part — flashing manically across the screen to the accompaniment of the trio's language music.

"I got five rings of paper, copier paper and two dead chickens and some buckets of acrylic, acrylic paint and I got a couple of students and we took over a studio and we just painted the chickens, pounded them on the paper, tore off a wing, painted it . . . pounded it on a couple of sheets of paper."

Wait, did he say "dead chickens?"

Yes, he did.

Turns out that although it's illegal (at least in New York state) to buy an unplucked chicken, Battaglia found a farm that would do it for him. "I had to do it really early in the morning. The farmer's wife went behind the barn and cracked the necks."

The entire film was made in about three hours. Three more hours were spent sitting around drinking coffee, "'cause we realized what we were going to do with these dead chickens (tearing them apart and everything and painting them) and that they smelled like, you know, chicken fat and stuff."

'Nuff said.

Following *Second Nature* (2000) —"My cartoon film" — and an unsuccessful attempt to make a computer film, *More True Shit* (2003), Battaglia returned to his pencils and made his master-work, *Crossing the Stream* (2006).

The premise of *Crossing the Stream* is as simple as they come: a man takes his horse across a stream. Yet, within that simple story is a magnificent, mind-blowing evocation of movement and spirituality. As the man and the horse hit the water, Battaglia takes us on a stoner/Zen trip; All consciousness is lost. Accompanied by the sounds of water and Tibetan singing bowls, water, animal, man, artist and viewer become one. It's like those moments when you're jogging (or driving, for you slackers) and you've run about half a mile, when you suddenly seem to wake and can't really remember the last half mile because you're so in tune with the movement and rhythm of your body: This is the experience of watching the scene in *Crossing the Stream*. As though hypnotized, you don't even realize it's happened until it's over. In the end, the man and the horse walk on and you wonder what the fuck that was all about and can you do it again, please?

Currently, Battaglia is finishing up a new film called *Car Crash Opera*. "It's 8 minutes. I want to criticize the car crash film by making a cartoon of it at first, but the second half of the film is after the car crash. The first 2 and a half minutes is developing the characters and then I got about a 2-minute car crash which is a lot of red pencil and ink, but then I've got this whole trail off of voices and it gets rather mournful. I want to criticize the form itself and then end with a little joke."

While Battaglia's films certainly fall into the realm of abstract or experimental animation, they're not cold, pretentious or devoid of personality; Battaglia's works are ambitious but always warm, personable and often funny. This is a man who enjoys his work and, more importantly, clearly enjoys life and extracts everything he can from it.

Figure 2.1　Aaron Augenblick

Figure 2.2　*Drunky*

Figure 2.3　*Plugs McGinniss*

CHAPTER 2

Aaron Augenblick
Last Exit to Brooklyn

There's never been a richer time in animation. With the emergence of new technologies that have made animation more affordable to produce and an animation boom that saw a rise in animation production on TV and the internet, in commercials, music videos, and in cinemas, the opportunity exists for animators to successfully straddle the line between commercial and artistic work. Brooklyn-based Aaron Augenblick is part of a growing trend of animators who operate small boutique studios that take on selective commissioned projects and then put their profits into creating personal short films.

Augenblick's background fittingly reflects his duo-animation citizenship; originally from Wilmington, Delaware, his father was a mechanical engineer and his mother an art teacher. "I feel like I am a perfect amalgam of these two schools of thought," says Augenblick. "I was raised with an appreciation for science and mechanical things, as well as a love of art and creativity. When I was a little kid, my dad built a robot arm called ORCA that is used to this day in chemical laboratories."

Augenblick was interested in animation at a very early age. "I had a crappy Apple IIe computer when I was a kid, with some primitive animation programs. My main character was a purple glob of goo who went on crazy adventures. They were very stupid, but I was doing my best to create funny stories like the ones I watched on TV."

It wasn't until high school though that Augenblick really felt that he could pursue a career in animation. While attending an animation summer course at the University of the Arts in Philadelphia, Augenblick tried traditional (drawn) animation for the first time. The experience changed his life. "When I saw my first pencil test it blew my mind. I made an old lady walking across the street with a walker. I had no idea what I was doing, so the old lady undulated and morphed into all kinds of crazy shapes as she walked. However, there was a life to the movement and the drawings that I had never encountered before and I knew I had to keep doing this and get better."

While majoring in animation at the School of Visual Arts (SVA) in New York, Augenblick made his first two films, *The Wire* (1996) and *Midnight Carnival* (1997). Augenblick's bold graphic and dark sensibilities are already present in the early black-and-white film *Midnight Carnival*. The protagonist — the Dignified Devil — is drinking alone in a bar. He finishes his drink, wanders the streets and then stumbles upon a lit doorway in an alley. He enters and discovers a strange carnival of freaks taking place. After walking through the carnival and seeing how one of the freaks sees him as a freak, the Devil remains and becomes part of the show.

After graduation, Augenblick took a breather from animation, but while working in Virginia as a night clerk in a hotel, MTV Animation came calling. "They had seen *Midnight Carnival* and asked me to work on the animated adaptation of the comic book *Hate* by Peter Bagge. I packed my stuff and came back to New

York and went to work." Augenblick ended up working for MTV on a variety of shows including *Hate*, *Daria* and *Downtown*, but by 1999 he was tired of doing hired work and wanted to go back to making his own films. "I wrote a script for an animated feature and showed it to a friend. He liked it so we pulled our money together and rented a small space in Brooklyn. I got a few more friends and we produced a 3-minute excerpt from the feature in an attempt to secure financing for the feature. That excerpt was *Ramblin' Man*. Unfortunately, we never got any funding, so we ran out of money fast. My partner left the studio and I was unable to continue paying any employees. I was at a very low point, with a failing studio and no idea what to do."

At that point, Augenblick decided that the best approach would be to combine freelance and independent work. "The idea was that I would be doing freelance work by day, while doing independent projects by night. This is when I think we became a real studio. I worked on a ton of freelance gigs, and also made *Drunky*, *Plugs McGinniss* and *The Dignified Devil*. Small jobs began to lead to bigger jobs and our first big break was *Shorties Watchin' Shorties* on Comedy Central. After that, I've had the luxury of being choosy about the freelance jobs we take on as a production studio. In addition, I have been able to develop my own projects like *Golden Age*."

Augenblick's first independent film was the striking *Ramblin' Man* (2000). In this short, a robotic cowboy and his horse on wheels ride to the Hank Williams tune. While there isn't much meat to the story, the visuals contain a stunning array of colors and original designs that clearly echo 1930s animation, in particular the work of the Fleischer Brothers and Ub Iwerks.

The film came from a dream sequence that Augenblick originally intended for a feature called *The Robot's Song*. "The story was about a circus-robot who runs away and finds love in the big city. I always loved Hank Williams, and this song was the perfect voice for the robot's dream of being a rootless drifter. We never got to make the full movie, but *Ramblin' Man* had a good life in animation festivals."

After finishing *Ramblin' Man*, Augenblick stumbled onto Flash animation (created using Adobe Flash software). When asked by a prospective employer if he knew the software, Augenblick lied and said that he did. "I learned it over a weekend, and started work on that Monday," remembers Augenblick. "I was amazed at how easy it was to create a fully realized cartoon. I had just finished *Ramblin' Man*, which was 3 minutes long and took about a year to make. My first Flash cartoon took about one week for the same amount of animation. I knew that even though it was a clumsy program, Flash was the key for my studio to create animation in a more feasible and economical way. Over the years, I have continued to evolve the way I use the program, to avoid using gimmicks and make more traditionally animated cartoons."

The Dignified Devil in Shirley Temple (2001) was an early experiment with Adobe Flash and a return to the main character of *Midnight Carnival*. It's not one of Augenblick's stronger films, but it is unique in that it offers a rare display of Augenblick's serious side. This time, the Devil protagonist wakes up in a hotel. Outside he sees twin girls fighting; he goes outside and ends up going after one of the troubled twins. They walk the streets together, talk and fuck. Then they sleep, she pukes on him and they go their separate ways. The story has a nightmarish David

Lynch tone to it (Lynch's work clearly influences Augenblick), but this strange moment between these two people is also grounded in reality. This blurring of nightmare and reality will become a common theme in Augenblick's work.

Another early Adobe Flash film was the hilarious *Drunky* (2002), which tells a rather unusual story of a straight guy who has sex with men when he gets drunk. Even at this early stage of Flash animation, Augenblick's bold visual style and innovative character designs immediately catch the eye and serve as the perfect complement to the distressed state of the main character. "I thought it would be funny if there was a straight guy who, whenever he got drunk, would black out and wake up having just had sex with a guy," adds Augenblick. "So, he would drink to deal with his emotional distress, and end up having sex with another guy again. A vicious circle. Then I added in the Disney angle (what's gayer than Disney?), having the antagonist be a classic Disney villain, complete with a 'Pink Elephants' style hallucination sequence."

2003 was a breakout year for Augenblick: during the year he completed a new short, *Plugs McGinniss* (about an alcoholic seeing-eye dog), a commissioned short called *The Man with the Smallest Penis* (about a man with a microscopic dick who finds love with a lab technician) and began work on a series for Comedy Central called *Shorties Watchin' Shorties* (2003–4). The series featured animated interpretations of stand-up routines from dozens of comedians including Dane Cook, Mike Birbiglia, Lewis Black, Bill Burr, Colin Quinn and Jim Gaffigan. "It was created by Eric Brown of World Famous Pictures," says Augenblick. "He was a fan of *Drunky* and contacted me to create animated content for the show. Basically, they would send us audio clips and we would find a funny way to animate them. We would have studio brainstorm sessions where everyone would come up with visual gags for the bits. It was a really fun time, and we produced a hell of a lot of animation."

After finishing *Shorties*, Augenblick landed another TV gig, this time for the MTV children's show parody, *Wonder Showzen*. When series creators John Lee and Vernon Chatman invited Augenblick to do the show's animation, they could not have found a more perfect fit for their twisted comic sensibilities. "It ended up being a match made in heaven. I still think *Wonder Showzen* was one of the best television shows of all time. The wide variety of styles we had to work in really pushed our limits, and made our studio much stronger artistically. It was always fun to get a new assignment from them and figure out how we were going to pull it off. We worked on *Wonder Showzen* for the two seasons it was on the air and it's still probably the work that we are best known for."

Augenblick directed all the shorts for the show and was given a long artistic leash. "They would send us a script, audio and rough designs and we would have a discussion about the overall direction," says Augenblick. "Sometimes they would have a very specific subject they were lampooning and other times it was more vague. Sometimes we would take it in a different direction they expected, but they were always encouraging us to be creative."

One of the standout shorts is *Mr. Bible*. Three characters representing sex, drugs and violence interrupt the nightly prayers of a sweet young child. Mr. Bible shows up to protect the boy but quickly finds himself drawn into the beliefs of the other characters. From that moment, all hell breaks loose as the Bible gets drunk, fucks the Koran and frees Jesus from the crucifix so that he can score with twins and break-dance in the church. The bit is not more than a minute long, but in that time Augenblick has created a hilarious and scathing satire of Christianity. Augenblick's inspired '30s-era animation adds a rich layer of irony to the piece: the young boy looks like a typical Disney character from that time, with his soft angelic features and gentle giant eyes. In the final scene, the break-dancing Jesus recalls the strange, rotoscoped Cab Calloway routine from The Fleischer Brothers short, *Snow White* (1933).

"*Mr. Bible* is one of my favorite *Wonder Showzen* bits," says Augenblick. "They wanted it to be in a '30s Fleischer style which is my personal favorite era of animation. We looked at a lot of old Betty Boop and Popeye cartoons and did our best to replicate that era. I always loved the weird rotoscoping that the Fleischers used to do, so we threw some in by having Jesus Christ do a little break-dancing at the end of the cartoon."

In 2006, Augenblick produced *Golden Age*, his finest work to date. Not surprisingly, the 22-minute faux documentary began its life as a commissioned series of episodes for Comedy Central. *Golden Age* is a masterpiece of parody that follows the scandalous lives of ten animated characters that have stumbled from stardom into a variety of misfortunes ranging from addiction to serial killings.

"*Golden Age*," says Augenblick, "started out as a pitch I wrote for a show about a retirement home for over-the-hill cartoon characters. Comedy Central was interested in it, but they felt the format was too similar to *Drawn Together*, which they were about to debut. They asked me if I could adapt the characters into a different format, and I hit upon the idea of presenting each character as a short documentary subject. They loved the idea, and commissioned us to do ten episodes. It was a really exciting project, because it allowed us to experiment with a wide variety of mixed-media and try a lot of things we had never done before."

Golden Age shows Augenblick expanding his graphic and storytelling skills. It's not often that an episodic piece of this length can sustain its energy, but Augenblick pulls it off with deft comic timing, rich character development (including many animation archetypes), and an array of techniques that masterfully mimic the animation of a character's time (from 1930s-era rubber hose animation to the limited, lame animation of the seventies and eighties). Augenblick's graphic approach is so informed and on the mark that *Golden Age* also serves as an impromptu history of animation techniques and styles.

"I'm a huge fan of animation history," says Augenblick, "and by the different styles and techniques animators have used in the past 100 or so years. I was lucky enough to be one of the last classes at SVA that had to learn how to use an Oxberry camera and that has informed a lot of the replications we've done of the old techniques."

The success of *Golden Age* and *Wonder Showzen* has brought Augenblick a steady stream of interesting work, including *Sesame Street* (a nifty piece about tall tales, featuring Johnny Cash), a short for comedian Louis C.K. and work on the ultra-violent, Gary Panter-influenced Adult Swim TV show *Superjail!* (2007).

What's remarkable about Augenblick's success is that no matter the type of work, his visual style is almost always recognizable and, more importantly, there's a common trait to all of his characters. Fusing the comic surrealism of the Fleischers with the nightmarish scenarios of David Lynch and the troubled, feeble characters of Hubert Selby Jr., Augenblick's protagonists are a messed-up bunch, struggling through absurd, haunting experiences, trying to find a semblance of identity and place.

Figure 3.1 Chris Landreth

Figure 3.2 *Ryan* 1

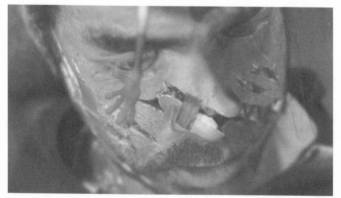

Figure 3.3 *Ryan* 2

CHAPTER 3

Chris Landreth's Psychorealism

Although computer animation has made gigantic strides during the last 20-plus years, it still remains crippled by uninspired concepts, plastic, hollow environments and cold and almost creepy character designs. Part of the problem is that animators (particularly students) spend so much time learning (and relearning) new technologies that the result is often rushed and incomplete. Many animators are at the mercy of the software — they let it lead them. With the bulk of their time spent dealing with the technical side, concepts seem to come last, hence the flood of generic garbage that is produced each year.

Canadian animator Chris Landreth is among the few computer animators creating strikingly original and intelligent films. Landreth's works are occupied by worlds and characters that initially seem surreal, but which transform into very real and disturbing insights into human psychology.

What's all the more remarkable about Landreth's story is that he was never much of an animation fan as a kid and only stumbled into the field in his twenties. "I had almost no interest in Saturday morning stuff when I was a kid," recalls Landreth. "I liked Rankin/Bass stop-motion stuff, you know, the Christmas specials. I suppose that got my attention. Not much else did. And then I went to school thinking I would be a scientist or an engineer. I went to undergraduate university and eventually graduate school."

It was during Landreth's first year of graduate school at the University of Illinois that animation caught his attention. "This computer graphics program started down the street from where I was doing my graduate studies and working. And although I really didn't want to go back to school again, it did seem kind of cool that I'd be able to perhaps hang out in this environment and either learn stuff through osmosis or actually get more committed. And I got to do that. I got to learn how to use Wavefront software."

During his computer studies, Landreth made a 2-minute film called *The Listener*. The film was invited to the prestigious computer animation festival Siggraph in 1991. Based on the film, Landreth was offered a job doing scientific visualization (using animation to visualize scientific data) at North Carolina Supercomputing Center (NCSC).

Landreth made two more films at NCSC: *Caustic Sky* (about the scintillating topic of acid rain formation) and *Data Driven: The Story of Franz K* (1993). Both films were accepted to Siggraph, but it was Landreth's 1993 trip to the festival that would change the course of his life. "A bunch of us from this North Carolina Supercomputing Center [were] down in Anaheim, California. We got [an] e-mail from the director of the home office, gleefully sending out e-mails saying that a massive restructuring was impending and that there was to be no need for a visualization group anymore. So we were all going to be out of a job. It so happened that we got that e-mail the afternoon of a huge party at Siggraph put on by Industrial Light and Magic. It was there that

I met people at Alias. And basically managed to work up terms of a job with them. Right then and there. They offered me a job as a, what they called, expert user. I started New Year's Day, 1994."

Alias Research was keen to get into the animation market. They hired programmers to make software, and Landreth's job was to use the software as it was being made.

"The deal that I was able to make with them," says Landreth, "was that I'd be happy to do that, but that they would need to trust me that I would want to do creative stuff, like make films."

Using software called PowerAnimator, Landreth's first "test-drive" was a film called *The End* (1995). Two wiry characters float and dance on a stage and pontificate to each other about life and art. Everything stops suddenly when a voice interrupts their performance/dialogue to inform them that they are characters created by an animator. The camera reveals the animator (who looks an awful lot like Landreth) and his storyboard for the film we've just watched, but after struggling to come up with an ending, the animator realizes that he is himself just another fictional character in this farce.

The End is a smart and rather scathing Pirandello-tinged parody of painfully pretentious experimental/abstract films that seem to speak to no one but the creator, and Landreth had a specific target in mind: computer animation. "The story itself is very much a parody of computer graphic films that had been coming out. There was such a degree of self-importance and all this lingo-speak that was developing. Interactivity started to become a big buzzword then, and that paradigms were shifting and that visual language was being created and stuff. So a lot of what those characters are saying at the beginning are actually mishmash I would lift from these treatises and academic papers and kind of screw around with."

The End was a marvel in the context of computer animation: here was a work that used innovative computer designs to actually tell a funny story with a solid concept. It also showed how computer animation, rather than drifting off into hallucinogenic or nerd landscapes and sci-fi worlds, could instead be used to look inward at humanity and the nature of art itself.

The End was an immediate success and earned Landreth an Academy Award nomination for Animation Short Film, putting him firmly on the list of animation artists to watch in the future.

Landreth didn't disappoint: he returned with *Bingo* (1998), a brilliant piece of satire taken from a theatre company in Chicago. "I grew up in Chicago," says Landreth. And my sister actually dragged me to come see this theatre company called the New Futurists. I was very resistant. But she dragged me out there. And I saw these guys perform, and I'd never seen anything like this. It's very interactive and improvisational and usually quite absurdist. Some of them are just spoken word monologues.

I'd clearly felt that I could take one of these performances verbatim and create an animation out of it. And so I talked with the director afterwards and introduced myself, and said I've really got to see as much of this material as you've got, either on video or I'll pore through this stuff live. And he sent me two or three hours of video footage of the plays just being performed live, raw."

Landreth was particularly interested in a short play they did called *Disregard this Play*. With permission from the theater group, Landreth took their performance and turned it into an animated film.

The lights shine on a meek young man in what appears to be an empty room. A clown enters and casually says, "Hi Bingo. Bingo the Clown." The man says that he's not Bingo, but the clown ignores him and continues to greet him as Bingo. Each time the clown speaks, his voice gets angrier and his physical appearance begins to change. A woman (dressed as a ringmaster) enters the scene and says, "music please." Circus music begins and a variety of strange monitors and figures appear out of nowhere. Other characters that emerge continue to aggressively insist that the man is Bingo. Finally, the poor, beaten guy gives up and readily admits that he is indeed Bingo the Clown.

Bingo is a masterpiece of absurdity complemented by stunning and original computer graphics and character designs that enhance the film's nightmarish dialogue and atmosphere. And where did Landreth find his inspiration for the visual look of the film? "It came," he says in all seriousness, "from a revulsion of clowns. I grew up in Chicago when there was John Wayne Gacy (the American serial killer who frequently entertained neighbourhood children dressed as a clown). He left a kind of a mark on a lot of people, including me, of how bad clowns can really be. So *Bingo* definitely hit a nerve there. Some beautiful ugly clowns came out of that whole memory and mishmash and stuff, and made its way into an environment that I'm very proud of. That environment was a very collaborative one, with this guy named Ian Hayden."

Bingo, however, is more than just a surreal visual farce. Landreth's own starting point for the film was the famous line by Joseph Goebbels: "If you tell a lie big enough and keep repeating it, people will eventually come to believe it." Even though the man knows the truth — he is not Bingo — after enough bullying and repetition, he forsakes his identity for that of the clown. On one hand, the quote is an obvious criticism of how the media and politicians mislead and manipulate the general population, yet it also shows us just how fragile we are in our skins. Rather than fight, the man takes the easy road. It's easier to just accept that he's Bingo than to fight for his true beliefs. Sadly, that's a reality that many of us know intimately.

And how did the theater director feel about Landreth's inter-pretation? "They were stunned," Landreth recalls. "I'm not sure what they made of it. I think he had a strong feeling of revulsion about it, but I'm okay with that."

Landreth spent a year and a half working on Bingo and says that it would have gone a lot quicker if the new software (Maya) didn't keep breaking down. "It was also extremely difficult to get support for it," adds Landreth.

"It's a software company and when they're in the throes of trying to write software by a deadline, could care less about this weird film that this guy is working on. But eventually I got it. And the film was released, actually, on the very same date that the software, Maya, was released."

Bingo would turn out to be Landreth's final work for Alias|Wavefront (Alias Research merged with Wavefront in 1995). "After I did *Bingo* and Maya was now the established piece of software, there was really no reason, as far as Alias was concerned for 6-minute-long films to be done. And I would have to agree with them from a business sense. There wasn't a need for that anymore. So I left in March of 2000."

Landreth wasn't out of work long — he took a very different

job with Nelvana (Toronto-based studio and one of the largest producers of children's television in the world) as the head of 3-D development. "I was taking directions from directors who wanted to develop 3D-stuff," says Landreth. "And I would oversee making these pilot short films for them. So I made two pilot short films. One was *Puff the Magic Dragon*, which no one will ever see — actually, they won't see both."

Things didn't pan out at Nelvana and he left the studio at the end of 2000; however, earlier that year, Landreth had an experience that would prove to change the course of his career and lead to the creation of one of most acclaimed animation films ever made.

This is where I momentarily enter the story: I invited Landreth to be on the selection committee of the Ottawa International Animation Festival along with three other animators. At the last minute, one of the people dropped out and I replaced him with an animator I had met in Montreal a few weeks earlier named Ryan Larkin. In the late sixties/early seventies, Larkin was one of the masters of animation. His Academy Award-nominated film, *Walking*, was considered one of the great works of animation. Sadly, his life took a tumble because of drugs, alcohol and mental health issues, and by the time I met him in June 2000, he was living in a Montreal mission and panhandling on the streets. After driving to Montreal to meet Ryan, I had thought it would be interesting to invite Ryan to our festival in September; however, when the opportunity arose, I thought it might be interesting to have Ryan be on the actual committee. I picked Ryan up in Montreal and brought him to Ottawa in July 2000.

Landreth remembers his unusual week with Larkin.

It was basically three of us, being the animation professionals, judging these films, and Ryan was at that point acting very much like a person who had not been around animation at all; very much like a bum, actually. He was saying, "I got to have my beer now . . . I'm tired, I got to lay down . . ." He was out of it for the first day or two. Then something kind of remarkable happened. He came to realize, I think, that he was in the company of people like he had been around when he was a creative person, and he started to really come alive, and we got to see him being lucid and engaged and very impassioned. That transformation of the personality was a very striking thing.

Then the last day, we showed each other our films. Ryan was the last, and he showed *Walking (1969)* and *Street Musique (1972)* and another film called *Syrinx (1965)*. We had seen the film *Walking* before, but now we were really looking at it. We came to realize that this person was a flaming genius in his time. We were looking at him today — and, first of all, what a change, what an incredible contrast . . . and then, second of all, as Derek [Lamb] in the film says, he's living out every artist's worst fear. But if this is where he's come to, there's something that's actually not horrible about that. There's something very redeeming.

I was immediately inspired to try to get that story into a film. I sat on that for a few months before acting on it. Then I decided that's what I wanted to do.

Landreth hooked up with Larkin again during the festival in September 2000. "While we were on the bus over to the [animators'] picnic I asked him, without any real premeditation, it was actually quite impulsive. He was on the bus with me. I said, what if I made a film about you, based on what I've known about you since I met you? He said, 'Sure.' But I did nothing about that until February 13, 2001."

In February Landreth approached Copperheart Entertainment producer Steven Hoban, who he'd worked with briefly on an IMAX project called *Cyberworld 3D.* "I remember," says Landreth. "He produced that, and wanted to include *Ryan* in that film and re-render it in 3-D — stereoscopic vision. And he was overruled at the time by Brad, the IMAX dude, who said that there'll be 4- or 5-year-old kids in the audience pissing in their seats if *Ryan* was included in that. But we stayed in touch, and he was completely on board from the very beginning, along with this other guy, Jeremy Edwardes. And a month later, I visited Marcy [Page] at the [National] Film Board. [The NFB came on board as co-producers in late 2002.]

During the spring and summer of 2002, Landreth headed to Montreal and spent over 20 hours conducting video and audio interviews with Larkin. Other than knowing that the film had to be Larkin being interviewed, Landreth didn't really have a specific direction at this stage. "The idea was vague at first," he says. "I was thinking along the lines of Nick Park's *Creature Comforts*, in which he interviewed people at a zoo in Bristol and then fashioned an animated film around the interviews."

Then came the turning point: at one point during the interviews, Landreth brings up Larkin's alcoholism. Landreth tells Larkin that he saw his own mother die from the disease and that he doesn't want to see Larkin follow the same path. Larkin, who'd been drinking heavily during the interview and was pretty much obliterated by this point, gets worked up by Landreth's question to the point where he explodes in anger. "It's obviously a big subject in Ryan's world," Landreth told *VFXWorld* magazine, "because he acts so impassioned and angrily toward it. But it is also a big subject in my world, too, and because of that, it brought the interviewer (me) way more into the story than I would have planned beforehand."

Landreth uses Maya software in the film and does an extraordinary job re-creating himself and Ryan (Larkin) as characters. The interview between the two takes place in an old, run-down cafeteria that looks like the waiting room for hell: an assortment of disfigured and literally broken characters occupy the space. Ryan's appearance is initially horrifying: Landreth has re-created him as a fragile, incomplete person — we see the remains of what was once a face, and much of Ryan's body is twisted, busted or just not there.

As Ryan reflects on his life, Landreth uses animation to create spaces and give psychological depth to the characters that simply would not be possible in live-action. In one poignant scene — and there are many, including the moment when Landreth pulls out original drawings from *Walking* and shows them to an emotional Larkin — we meet Felicity, Ryan's old girlfriend. Seeing the two of them speaking "face to face" about what might have been is powerful, heartbreaking stuff. When Ryan places his hand on Felicity's, I dare you to keep your eyes dry. His memories of their happy times together momentarily turn him into a younger, "complete" Ryan, with hippie threads and long hair, who comes to life in his award-winning film *Street Musique*. He is filled with joy and soon begins dancing with his creations.

Perhaps it's because of my intimacy with the subject, but I

found the aforementioned alcohol scene difficult to watch — I mean that in a good way. At one point, Landreth (now wearing a halo of sorts) brings up Ryan's alcoholism; Ryan, the calm, reflective, scared little boy, is caught off guard. He claims that his beers are all that he has left — he doesn't want to become a tea drinker. Landreth tells him that he just wants to see him stay alive and return to filmmaking. Suddenly Ryan erupts: he stands up and takes on the appearance of a demon with red spikes protruding from his face. Ryan berates everyone and no one for his state: everyone had robbed him, and without money he has nothing. An intimidated Landreth backs off, his halo explodes and he wonders why he prodded Ryan to begin with.

The scene is powerful, mature and tense stuff — something you don't see much of in animation these days. The combination of Landreth's inventive character design and the raw awkwardness that you could only get through a real, unscripted interview gives this scene an intensity that is rare in animation. *Ryan* offers no affected, grand philosophical musings, no soppy poetic histrionics. This is life with all its dank, dark, dirty warts; this is the story of a real life gone astray. I don't mean just Ryan's life either: Landreth is drawn to Ryan because he sees aspects of his own life and family in Ryan.

Ryan is a film about failure. There is no happy ending. Landreth realizes that Larkin will not change and the film ends with Larkin back working the street. But there is a glimmer of hope: Ryan (who died in February 2007) may not have changed, but he seems to trigger change in people who knew him. "In some ways," says Landreth, "I look at his life, and there's something very reassuring about it. He's basically followed Murphy's Law [if something can go wrong, it will] as an artist. If you look at his life now — yeah, he's poor, he's sort of on the bottom rung of society — but, on the other hand, he has in many ways a very positively structured life. He has a community of dozens of people who, if they don't know that he is an artist, at least know that he's a decent guy, and they take care of him. He has a community of people that a lot of us would find enviable."

Ryan was a massive success on the festival circuit and took home the Academy Award for Animation Short Film in 2005. Landreth became an instant star in the film world (both the live-action and animation circuits) and was invited to give lectures and discuss the film. He also received offers to make feature films, but instead, Landreth decided to make a short film called *The Spine* (2009).

"It's about an extremely dysfunctional marriage," says Landreth. "It follows the trajectory, over a short period of time, of a marriage between Dan and Mary. It's going to play tragedy against comedy. It's going to start off in this kind of darkly comic tone that, say, *Bingo* would have. It's very oppressively absurdist. Dark tone. So, yeah, I'm going to do this with this film and see how it goes."

Whatever the future holds for Landreth, his reputation is secured as one of the most inspiring, original and provocative animation artists around.

Figure 4.1   Evan and Greg Spiridellis

Figure 4.2   *JibJab: The Early Years*

Figure 4.3   *JibJab: This Land*

CHAPTER 4

JibJab

Redefining the Toon

In July 2004, just before releasing their latest internet short, *This Land*, Evan and Gregg Spiridellis were beginning to wonder if success would ever find them. Although JibJab, their studio of four and a half years, had overcome obscurity, survived the dot-com crash of 2000 and produced a couple of modest internet animation hits, they still weren't sure if producing animation for the internet would ever be a profitable venture. Their answer was fast, surreal and unprecedented.

This Land, a parody of the 2004 presidential election, was released on 9 July, 2004. By the end of the election, over 80 million people had viewed the film (and the follow-up film, *Good to Be in DC*); the films were seen on every continent. After FOX News interviewed the Spiridellis brothers, the real madness began. Every major media outlet in the US came calling; the brothers were guests on *The Tonight Show with Jay Leno*. "NASA," according to Evan Spiridellis, "even called us to request a copy to send the American astronaut on the international space station!" To top it all off, the Spiridellis brothers were named "People of the Year" by Peter Jennings of ABC News.

No independent animation film in history has tasted that kind of success. Not bad for a company that started in a Brooklyn garage.

"I have been interested in animation for as long as I can remember," says Evan, "although I can't say I was actually "aware" of it until a few years after I graduated college. I was always good at drawing from the time I was little and I loved making pictures so I always knew I would pursue art in some capacity, I just didn't realize it would ultimately lead me towards animation."

Like so many independent animators, Evan took the roundabout route to animation; he studied illustration at Parsons the New School for Design and didn't make animation until after he graduated. One of Evan's Professors at Parsons, David Passalacqua, put him on the road towards animation. "Dave's philosophy," recalls Evan, "was that drawing was at the heart of *everything*. Dave encouraged constant experimentation and change so drawing and painting led me to photography and puppet making."

In 1998, while living in Brooklyn and doing animation and illustration, Evan had an idea for a television show — at that time, Gregg had left his banking job and moved to Philadelphia to get his MBA — and it was during a visit to Philadelphia that their career paths moved closer together. "My wife (girlfriend at the time) and I went down to visit Gregg and he played an animation by John [Kricfalusi, creator of *The Ren and Stimpy Show*] of a dancing doodie that was streaming through a 28K modem. We were talking about my TV idea and I will never forget when he said to me, 'Do you really want to be banging out horseshoes while the Model T is rolling off the assembly line?' That was my 'Eureka!' moment. There were a million artists trying to get their TV pitches onto the air and here was a brand new, completely undefined medium just waiting to get filled up."

What was particularly appealing to the brothers was the freedom that the internet offered: it was uncharted territory so they had a chance to stand out more than they would in traditional mediums, and they would also have direct contact with their audience — there would be no producers, distributors and assorted middlemen. More importantly, by the late 1990s, new technologies afforded independent artists the possibility to create quality work faster. "The opportunity to build a new kind of media company was too big for us not to jump on," says Evan. "So when Gregg graduated school he moved up to Brooklyn and we started JibJab."

From the start, the brothers had a distinct collage-esque visual style that helped them stand out from the growing internet animation pack. "Our collage look was really born out of technical limitations," says Evan. "We did our first collage piece back in February 2000 and at that time 99 percent of internet content was still delivered through a 28 or 56K modem so we had to keep our files small. We were using Macromedia Flash to produce all our shorts and the way the software worked was that once you downloaded an asset it could be used over and over again in the file without having to download the data on every frame. At the time, everybody was producing vector graphics because they were so tiny but we figured we could load bitmap images into these symbols just as easily and it would give us a unique look."

In 2000, JibJab had their first hit with an animated political satire called *Capitol Ill*. The crudely animated collage parody features George W. Bush and Al Gore debating with each other in rap rhymes. *Capitol Ill* was viewed online and JibJab was showcased on ABC News, CNN and FOX. MADtv then licensed the piece for their pre-election show.

Just as business was running smoothly, the dot-com crash arrived and torched virtually the entire internet animation industry. Amazingly (ain't these guys full of fortune?), JibJab managed to survive the crash. "Gregg saw the dot-com crash coming at least six months before the bubble burst," says Evan, "so we started to explore new opportunities that would enable us to avoid having to get 'real jobs'! During that time we sold and manufactured novelty toys, wrote and illustrated children's books and would take on the occasional advertising or corporate gig to fill up the JibJab coffers."

Service work kept JibJab afloat and helped them maintain a staff of about a dozen people; however, the brothers didn't start JibJab to work for others, so in 2002 they moved to California. "We lived in the Travelodge by the LAX airport for ten days while we found new apartments and a place to work," recalls Evan. "We set up shop in a dressing room on a studio lot and cut our costs so that we were able to weather the storm and keep on trucking."

Meanwhile, JibJab continued to make political satires. In 2003, they made *Founding Fathers*, which features the Founding Fathers of the US Constitution rapping, followed by the hilarious *Ahnuld for Governor*. In this parody of California governor candidate and movie star Arnold Schwarzenegger, the (cough-cough) "actor" lists off his many important experiences that he feels can help California, but sadly, they all come from his movies.

Then came *This Land*. Using Woody Guthrie's seminal song, George W. Bush and Democratic presidential candidate John

Kerry hurl a string of insults at each other during their race to make our land their land.

While JibJab's parodies are innovative and funny, they are, ultimately, political-satire light. This is not heavy political commentary and JibJab makes no apologies for that; the studio has consciously taken a middle ground, content to rip into both parties with equal venom. "We keep our personal political opinions *out* of our work," admits Evan. "Our main objective when we produce anything, political satire included, is to make as many people laugh and to do that we try to point out the absurdities that exist on both sides of any given argument. While I'm sure there's a small percentage of people that might look down on us and say we're squandering an opportunity to really *say* something I feel like there are enough political pundits shouting their opinions from the rooftops and our objective is to give people a break from it."

With the success of *This Land*, JibJab received a stream of offers, but few that interested them. "We were the flavor of the month in Hollywood and pretty much all the doors that we'd been banging on opened up to us. The only difference was that at this point we weren't too interested in doing traditional media anymore. We were offered multiple film and TV deals but weren't eager to put our fate in the hands of a big media company." The brothers simply felt that, while no one quite knew yet how to make any money off internet films, JibJab did have enormous distribution without having to answer to anyone. Creative freedom was of far greater value to JibJab than any of the offers they received. "After four and a half years in business and weathering some very lean years," says Evan, "we both felt like it was time to double down and concentrate on the web rather than fold our cards and put our fate in the hands of the big studios."

Despite their success, JibJab was very conscious of ensuring that the studio didn't become compartmentalized as political satire animators. "While I love political humor and collage animation," adds Evan. "We never want to be pigeon holed into one form of storytelling or one visual style. We'll always continue to do collage animation and political humor but I also love puppetry and stop-motion and live-action and just about *any* visual medium that fits the story we're trying to tell. I have too much fun experimenting to settle into just one way of doing things."

JibJab have certainly stayed true to their word: they have created more interactive content, like JibJab Sendables eCards, which are little movies based on various themes and holidays. A unique component of these eCards is "Starring You!" — this enables the viewer to pick a theme and upload head images of themselves, family or friends directly into the film. Creating a new avenue of expression not only veered JibJab away from the political satire corner, but it also covered their butts if one of their new films flopped. "We were launching a new piece every three or four months," says Evan, "and without fail we would get 3–5 million views in the first four weeks out of the gate. Those numbers put us consistently on par with the #1 video on YouTube yet there wasn't really a business there and the pressure of having to produce a 'hit' every time we stepped up to bat was making us really uncomfortable. In addition we've premiered 11 shorts on *The Tonight Show with Jay Leno* and we've gotten a good amount of press but we knew that one of these days we'd produce a dud and we were scared everything we'd built would just go away."

The thinking behind Sendables eCards evolved out of JibJab's belief that their work was connecting with audiences because they were dealing with collective experiences like elections or year-in-reviews. The downside of these events is that they only come around every so often, so JibJab wanted to find something more familiar and frequent and, well, birthdays and holidays seemed like a pretty damn obvious fit. When Gregg approached him with the idea, Evan was initially reluctant. "My immediate reaction," recalls Evan, "was 'I am not turning JibJab into an e-card company!' and I was adamant about it. Then, once I stopped thinking about it in terms of what currently exists, I saw a massive opportunity. The moment you lose the stigma of being an 'e-card' and just say I'm gonna create a funny 20-second video about a birthday it not only becomes really manageable but really fun, too."

JibJab launched the Sendables eCards "Starring You!" films in April 2007. JibJab had actually tried to do something similar back in 2000, but they found themselves ahead of the technology of the time. There are currently over 30 "Starring You!" films. Over 10 million people have "made" films and another 45 million have viewed the films. These are numbers that likely outdo the combined viewing audiences of many of the famous indie animators!

Considering how innovative and successful JibJab has been during the last decade, it will be interesting to see how the studio evolves in the future. As new formats emerge, new forms of storytelling continue to develop. "We're very, very excited about the future of the studio and internet content in general. New formats will emerge and it will take an entirely new generation or artists and storytellers to define the medium."

Evan compares the digital situation today to the arrival of television and how many movie producers at the time worried that it would kill off their business. "Instead what happened was that new types of storytelling formats emerged: sitcoms, game shows, nightly news — these are now all part of our daily lives and things that we take for granted but they simply didn't exist 50 years ago. The web is in the exact same place right now."

If anyone is in a position to radically redefine the way we watch animation, it seems JibJab is. "There's a very big opportunity for guys like us and an entirely new generation of artists that are coming up," says Evan. "Trying to figure all this stuff out is just as exciting and rewarding as actually making short films."

Figure 5.1   PES on set of *Sprint* shoot

Figure 5.2   *The Fireplace*

Figure 5.3   *Roof Sex*

CHAPTER 5

PES Play

Okay, first things first: what's with the PES name? With the exception of Dutch animator Rosto A.D., there aren't many animators around using nicknames. Animators are for the most part a pretty low-key group of folks. "Pes is a family nickname. It comes from my last name, Pesapane [his first name is Adam], which Americans have a terrible time pronouncing or writing correctly. I once received mail addressed to 'Propane.' It's just easier this way — PES . . . except in a noisy bar, where people tend to hear the word PISS."

And no, it ain't after the candy — that's PEZ. This is PES (rhymes with Les, as in Les Nessman from *WKRP in Cincinnati*). Still, the thing is that PES's work is very much like candy, or eye candy. The New York animator sticks out from the crowd with strikingly original and playful stop-motion works that use everyday objects and put them in an entirely new context; for example, in PES's *The Fireplace* — the world's first animated instant TV fireplace — he uses pretzels and candy corn to create a roaring fake fire for those cold nights in your hearthless home). All the more impressive is the fact that, like Aaron Augenblick, PES has managed to successfully straddle the border between commercial and independent work without giving up his artistic integrity.

Born in Dover, New Jersey, PES says that he was always

interested in art. "I learned how to paint watercolors at an early age. But I was also an athlete; I played soccer and tennis and excelled at both, so that definitely offset any ribbing that I may have taken simply as the 'artist' of the class."

After studying English literature and printmaking at the University of Virginia, PES got a rather uninspiring job at an advertising agency in New York. Using his ample free time, PES watched various music videos, commercials and short films that the agency received and became inspired to make his own films. And that's precisely what he did, but there was one minor problem: PES didn't know anything about filmmaking. "Basically I had to figure out how to make the thing myself," says PES. "I never went to school for film, so I didn't know anything about cameras. I borrowed a 16mm camera (a cheap Russian camera called the Krasnogorsk) from some guy at the agency who was too busy with his day job to use it. I took it home on the weekends and shot rolls of 16mm reversal film, experimenting with lenses, etc. I got my hands on an old 16mm projector and watched the dailies against the white wall in my bedroom. This is how I learned to use a camera."

His first film, *Dogs of War* (1998), shows kids playing in a field when abruptly their serenity is interrupted by the sound of bomber planes. The kids flee in terror — or do they? Turns out they're racing to catch falling hot dog wieners.

While the film was shot in live-action, it already anticipates PES's animation work through the use of absurd humor, placing everyday objects in unfamiliar situations and slick editing that clearly shows an influence of advertising films.

Dogs of War was based on "a surreal dream of bombers dropping hot dogs on Dresden." PES used his "free" time at the agency to draw storyboards, tinker with the concept and solicit feedback from his colleagues. Once he felt comfortable with the story structure, he started to make the film, but it was then that he discovered another stumbling block: money. PES wanted to use authentic WWII bombing footage, but realized that the licensing fees would cost — wait for it — a bomb, so he came up with another idea. "I called a military stock footage house, pitched the head of the company my idea, and asked if he could help me out by donating some specific footage. He did. A week later I got the high res tape in the mail."

It shouldn't come as a surprise that, although they come from very different times and worlds, the first animator to really knock PES on his ass was Jan Svankmajer, the Czech surrealist master well known for his object animation. "In 1997," recalls PES, "I stumbled into a screening of Svankmajer's feature film *Conspirators of Pleasure* at the Film Forum in New York City. I remember being impressed first and foremost by the lack of dialogue in the film. That was really exciting for me. I was also intrigued by the random bits of object animation sprinkled throughout the picture."

After the screening, PES headed out to find Svankmajer's films on video and was blown away by the work. "I studied it frame by frame. It opened a real door of perception for me about what could be done by moving objects around. It wasn't long before I had some ideas of my own."

While PES had drawing skills, he found that object animation was more appealing because it allowed him to work faster by bringing, as he says, "ideas to life without having to first worry about drawing these objects or rendering and texturing them. It was just grab it and go. I liked how it took the focus off the act of recreating an object and instead placed it on what ideas you can generate with that object."

By the time PES started on his first animation film, *Roof Sex* (2002), he had quit the advertising agency to focus solely on film-making. "When I had the idea for *Roof Sex*," says PES, "I basically didn't want anyone to fuck it up, so I decided to teach myself how to animate. The idea of hiring another animator never entered my mind — I just thought, I have this idea, let me figure out how to make it. I ordered doll furniture from eBay and did tests on my dining-room table. Then I quit my job because I knew it would be impossible to hold a day job while shooting this film."

The premise of *Roof Sex* is, well, relatively straightforward: two chairs head up to the rooftop of a New York building and fuck each other silly. The idea to make a furniture porn film came to PES after he stumbled upon a furniture porn website.

"It had simple still photos of chairs having sex, assembled as a joke," says PES. "I took one look at this idea and thought, here's a killer app for stop-motion."

On the surface, *Roof Sex* looks like a film that was tossed off rather quickly, but PES worked on developing the idea for almost a year. "I started with the simple idea of two chairs having sex. I wrote dozens of possible scripts, looking for one that really excited me. I considered dozens of locations and plot details. I drew lots of pictures, trying to work things out."

Roof Sex, like *Dogs of War*, uses fast-paced editing and keeps the viewer guessing until the last possible moment. Both of these approaches clearly show the impact advertising was having on

PES's work. "I took from commercials the idea of ending on the last possible moment with a surprise twist. Keep a viewer hooked till the last moments of the film — the very last second, if possible — then BANG! I find real power in it. It's one of the most important things I learned from advertising."

After completing the film, PES posted *Roof Sex* online and e-mailed it to some friends. Two weeks later, he had a weird experience: "I was in a bar and overheard a couple people talking about it. That was a trippy moment. I definitely had the sense that I had created something that connected with people on a mass scale."

Just as PES was ready to put *Roof Sex* aside and move on to his next film, his girlfriend and eventual partner, Sarah Phelps, pushed him to submit the film to festivals. Initially, PES wasn't so keen. "Film festivals? I didn't care about them; I never saw that as a venue for my films. I thought it was a ridiculous concept to think about people in a theater watching a 1-minute film. I still feel this way."

Sarah felt differently and took charge, getting *Roof Sex* out to festivals. They applied to many festivals and were accepted by the Annecy animation festival in France. PES had no idea how special it was to be accepted into the world's largest and oldest animation festival. "It was supposedly a big deal in the animation world, so we went. I remember all I wanted to do in Annecy was go for a bike ride in the French countryside and go eat cheese from that cow down the street. Sitting in a dark theater was the last thing in the world I wanted to do. My lone animation goal at Annecy was to meet Svankmajer, who was having a show in the castle. (I did meet him). In general, I was 100 percent ignorant of the animation world and just happy to have a free trip."

Even when *Roof Sex* won the Best First Film award, PES still didn't clue in to what this meant. "I was amused by the kind of reception *Roof Sex* received. All these people wanted to meet me? For what? I moved two chairs back and forth on a rooftop for three months. Most people would call that person an idiot."

When the "idiot" got home, the film's achievement finally sunk in: his fax machine was flooded with requests from buyers who had seen the film at Annecy; there were contract offers; there was money. PES finally realized that being seen at a film festival had value. Distributors and buyers came to festivals looking for films. This was good. Money meant that PES could make more films — or so he thought.

Even with licensing fees for *Roof Sex*, PES found himself $50,000 in debt. "I had used eight credit cards to finance my first five films and the licensing money barely covered my living expenses in NYC. The credit card companies refused to give me another card. I had given up my day job at the ad agency so I could make these films, but now I had no money coming in. I had hoped that the length of my films — all a minute or less — would get me a chance to direct commercials. I knew this would be a way for me to climb out of debt. Unfortunately no one would hire me yet."

At this point, PES decided to make even simpler, shorter films or, as he calls them, "short shorts." Using a digital camera, he started making films in his apartment using whatever objects he found lying around. One item he found particularly appealing was a peanut. "The peanut became a bit of obsession. I found it an incredibly useful and interesting object. I didn't grow up thinking my destiny was crossed with the peanut or anything, it was just something I grabbed one day and started using."

PES made a series of short shorts then eventually turned the peanut obsession into a longer film called *Pee-Nut*. A fish swims peacefully in the water; a stream of piss, courtesy of a peanut penis, disrupts the swim and then knocks a fly into the water; the fish eats the fly; the pissing stops; all is well in the world. The story is simple, but no one goes to see PES films for Faulkner narratives: The richness of PES's work is in the originality and beauty of the visuals. The meaning is in the images. Aside from the penis made out of peanuts, PES uses a dazzling old purse (which was cut open) for the water and, appropriately, a fish pendant for the fish.

"I took this lowbrow, scatological thing and literally cloaked it in gold," adds PES. "I loved the idea of dressing up something as base as piss and making it a thing of beauty. For some reason I am drawn to this sort of highbrow/lowbrow contrast. Plus I liked the idea of taking something quintessentially masculine — the target-practice piss — and creating it with things women often use as fashion items: gold necklaces, diamonds, pendants, pins, sequin purse fabrics. With *Pee-Nut*, I was discovering I could imbue an idea with multiple shades of meaning, associations, and insinuations — and even draw some unexpected humor out of things — by my selection of objects."

Around this time, PES and Phelps had an electrical fire in their apartment. "The sockets started smoking one day and I lost a lot of equipment in this power surge — a stereo, clock radio, microwave, etc. Before I took this stuff out to the garbage I tore into it with a hammer and removed all the circuit boards. I laid them on the kitchen table and saw immediately it looked like a city from an aerial perspective."

For several months, PES built a city using salt and peppershakers, old flashlights and other objects. Once the city was done, PES didn't really know what to do with it; the model just collected dust in a corner of the apartment until one day PES decided to get rid of the thing. It was at that moment, an idea struck: "Why not craft a film around the act of destroying it?" The result was *KaBoom!* (2004) — one of PES's strongest and most successful films.

A city is on alert as a bomber plane attacks. From here, PES's visual magic takes over: we see clown heads on machine guns, popcorn bullets, missile matches, exploding gift-wrap ribbons, peanut bombs and a final attack that sees the city annihilated Christmas tree balls. *KaBoom!* is a visual feast that cleverly appropriates images of peace (notably Christmas decorations) for the purposes of war. Is it a subtle comment on religious violence, an anti-Christmas film or just the inspired imaginings of a man who remembers what it is to be a child? Every kid has — okay, most boys have — played war games with their toys. Through their senses, war becomes fun, exciting and even pleasant. *KaBoom!* is just that: a vision of war through the animated eyes of a child.

KaBoom! had originally been a 30-second piece called *Atomic Nut*. It started, PES says, as "just another peanut film." Then he got a call from the clothing company Diesel. They asked him to be part of their Diesel Dreams ad campaign. "What they asked for," recalls PES, "was this: a minute long film, the best idea I could give them, delivered by such and such a date to an office in Amsterdam, with no questions asked. It was carte blanche, anything I wanted, no one to answer to creatively but myself. This has never happened to me again (as far as commercial work is concerned)."

It got even better. Not only would PES get paid to make the film, but he'd also be able to keep the ownership rights. PES saw this as a golden opportunity and certainly the biggest commercial break of his career. "Diesel was one of edgiest, best advertisers in the world," says PES. "Their commercials were legendary. What they were offering me was basically free distribution of the *one* idea I wanted to put out there in the world more than any other. As long as I came through with one of the standout films of this 30-film collection, I was guaranteed to make a mark in the commercial world."

PES added 30 seconds to the front of *Atomic Nut* and renamed it *KaBoom!* It was an immediate sensation; it went online in August 2004 and has received over a million hits.

KaBoom! was the hit of the Diesel films chosen for the campaign and PES started receiving commercial scripts from around the world. He'd make his mark.

PES has since done a number of commercials, but two in particular stand out: *Coinstar* (2005) and *Human Skateboard* (2007). *Coinstar*, a 60-second piece made to promote a coin machine, features coins that have been lost or forgotten in a house and are all heading to a living room table; once there, the coins, in a clever bit of animation, stack together to make a lady's shoe.

"I believed the idea was better suited to 60 seconds (it was originally commissioned as a 30-second piece)," adds PES, "and pitched the agency an approach that involved building out the back end of the film, the 'stacking sequence' which was not in the original script. I felt it was important, once the coins made it to the final table, that we didn't just magically cut to a finished shoe but actually explored the process by which the hundreds of coins came together. Aside from making the coin shoe feel much more impressive, this stacking sequence — unlike the rest of the spot — was something that people hadn't seen before."

With *Human Skateboard*, made for Sneaux shoes, PES took a somewhat different approach and used stop-motion animation of real people: one guy as the skateboarder, another as the skateboard.

"This was the best concept I have ever seen from an advertising agency," says PES. "In four years of directing commercials this is the only time I looked at a script and was wowed by an idea. It felt more like a personal project than a commercial to me, like something I'd wake up and make on my own."

The only significant change that PES made to the piece was to shift the focus from the skateboarder to the skateboard. "There is not a single close-up of the rider. I felt the success of the commercial would be in direct proportion to how much viewers *felt* the pain and the exhilaration of the human skateboard."

By 2006, PES found himself suddenly saturated with the riches of commercial work and desiring to make his own film again. "On commercials it's easy to get spoiled as a director," says PES. "There's someone to do everything for you. All you have to do is ask and it's taken care of. *Game Over* (2006) was a personal challenge. I wanted to prove to myself that I could make a good film without relying on anyone else. I locked myself in a room for two months and did it. It's the only film I have ever done entirely on my own."

Inspired by an interview with Pac-Man creator Toru Iwatani — who said he got the idea from a pizza that was missing a slice — PES recreates vintage video games like Space Invaders and Pac-Man using his arsenal of objects. Like *KaBoom!*, *Game Over* toys with high- and lowbrow themes. It's another PES film inspired by childhood, but it's also tinged with a pinch of darkness: no matter how far you go in a game, you will always die. "Death is what I remembered most about gaming in the eighties. For me it was all about the one enemy who got you every time, not about the tens of thousands of invaders you killed successfully."

Now, if that ain't a metaphor for, well . . . you know . . . that crazy word called existence than I don't know what to tell ya. The message is simple: life's a game. Explore it. Enjoy it.

PES's most recent film, *Western Spaghetti* (2008) shows that, despite a reliance on the visual, he's still armed with some solid concepts. This time he takes on the task of making a spaghetti dinner — with, of course, objects replacing the food. Unlike his previous films, *Western Spaghetti* lacks that wallop of an ending: there's no surprise because we know where the film is heading — a spaghetti dinner. Instead, the film's humor and pleasure come from the unexpected, yet somehow fitting, choices that PES makes for the objects. Pick-up sticks replace the spaghetti, bubble wrap becomes boiling water, foil paper turns into oil and, most unusually, Post-it Notes become the butter.

Now, there's "Western" in the title, but no sign of Italian cowboys or Sergio Leone references, so what is the Western all about? "The 'Western' in the title," says PES, "refers to the endless supply of worthless, modern junk that populates so much of our world. Google eyes, rubber bands, tinfoil, bubble wrap, keychain Rubik's Cubes, etc. It's all stuff most people are trying to throw away. There is beauty to be found in these objects."

PES's work reminds me of hanging out with my kids: they're juvenile, childish, magical, fun, repetitive, intelligent, perceptive, stupid, cute, vicious and silly. I wouldn't want it any other way. Sadly, the kids will grow up; let's hope that PES doesn't.

Figure 6.1   Patrick Smith

Figure 6.2   *Delivery*

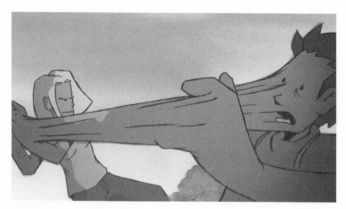

Figure 6.3   *Handshake*

CHAPTER 6

Patrick Smith's Twisted Catastrophes

New York animator Patrick Smith is like the Bono of indie animation
— minus the annoying glasses, self-righteousness, political com-
mentaries and Irish accent. Actually, he's nothing like Bono. It's
just that he seems to be everywhere: whether he's got a film or not,
he's always at animation festivals; if there's an article about indie
animation, you're sure to find a quote from Smith; he teaches and
gives lectures; he writes a blog about animation; he helped create
two very fine DVD collections of the New York animation scene
(*Avoid Eye Contact*) and just always seem to be out there talking
up his animation and others. It's an admirable trait that Smith
has clearly borrowed from animators like Bill Plympton and Don
Hertzfeldt. Smith realizes that the film doesn't end once you've
finished making it: you've got to then get the film out there to
people — submit to festivals, create websites and blogs, and, in
general, talk it up. Some of the more precious indie animators
frown on self-publicity: they feel it's beneath them, but the reality is that promotion and distribution is all part of the artistic
process. If indie animators don't shout their work out, who else
is gonna do it?

"By doing a lot of solid, effective self-promotion," adds Smith,
"you increase the number of people that see your work. Art and
animation has always been about communicating an idea for

me, and the more people that I talk to, the better. Bill and Don are masters. Some more arty types look down on them for their salesmanship, but at the end of the day, it allows them to make the films they want to make."

Oddly enough, if things had gone the way the Puerto Rican-born Smith had originally hoped, animation would never have been on the cards. "My brother Tom was always the artist in the family, he ended up as a nursing home administrator. I was left to do things on my own, but always supported by my parents who were amateur art collectors, surrounding us with art my entire childhood. I spent most of my time skateboarding, and when I wasn't doing that I was drawing skateboardesque graphics, trying my best to duplicate the style of legendary graphic designer for Santa Cruz Skateboards, Jim Phillips."

After his career in skate- and snowboarding was cut short by injuries, Smith was wandering about the University of Massachusetts Amherst (UMass) library one day and he noticed a book called *The Illusion of Life: Disney Animation*, by Frank Thomas and Ollie Johnston. This seminal book about the Disney animation process changed Smith's life.

"Everything changed." recalls Smith. "I wanted to be an artist, and animation was the medium that grabbed my attention. It wasn't the content of the Disney stories that amazed me, rather it was the execution and refined technique. When I first saw animated films like *The Wall* or revisited my childhood favourite *Fantasia*, I realized that animation was capable of way more than mere entertainment for children. The last nail in the coffin was my exposure to independent animation and the likes of Danny Antonucci, Bruno Bozzetto and Bill Plympton. I was hooked."

After his animated discovery, Smith dropped out of UMass and applied to the California Institute of the Arts (CalArts) — home to one of the world's best-known animation departments. Rejected, Smith returned to UMass in the painting department. "The professors allowed me to study animation on my own, mostly from books," says Smith. "They didn't really know how to help me, but they allowed me to complete a film as my bachelor of fine arts thesis project."

Following graduation, Smith went to bat at CalArts again. Strike two. The same day he was rejected, however, he received a call from MTV Networks: they liked the pencil test that Smith had sent them and invited him to produce a 10-second TV channel identification. "It was a video pencil test of a series of heads opening to reveal more heads," remembers Smith. "It was abstract since I didn't know how to draw yet." The spot won a Broadcast Design Association award and a prize at the 1995 Holland Animation Film Festival. MTV offered Smith a job doing layout on *Beavis and Butt-Head*. He accepted and moved to New York.

If Smith couldn't find a school willing to teach him animation, then he'd learn by doing it himself. "I wanted to be taught," says Smith, "but really, nobody would teach me. I went about it, at first, digesting books, mostly technique books like Tony White's book *The Animator's Workbook* or the classic book by Preston Blair."

Then Smith learned, as so many animators did before the days of animation schools, that the best way to learn animation is to just get out there and do it. "It's amazing," adds Smith, "how many animators sit around and don't animate. I animated a lot and learned tons by doing so. I made every mistake in the book, and discovered some things on my own that someone probably could have taught me in a fraction of the time, but I kind of like that I carved it out myself."

Working in New York animation studios didn't hurt Smith's cause either. "I did every job that came up and I concentrated on working with the veteran animators. Back then, I had a running collection of photocopied notes from legends like Glen Keane, Tissa David, and Eric Goldberg. From these notes I learned a lot of the basics of movement, story boarding, and design."

Smith spent two years learning the craft and then hit the road for Indonesia to do "nothing but surf, doodle and play backgammon" for a year. Upon his return to New York, MTV hired him to direct their new shows *Downtown* and *Daria*. At the same time, Smith started animating his own film, *Drink* (2000).

A young man pours himself a drink and swallows it; instantly, assortments of people — young and old, of different genders, classes and religions — begin to emerge from out of the man's mouth. Finally the chain ends with the young man re-emerging at the top of this long ladder of people. He takes another drink and order — or at least the illusion of it — is restored.

For a young, relatively inexperienced animator, *Drink* is quite a beginning. Using the seemingly simple and mundane action of taking a drink, Smith creates a funny and creepy philosophical piece on the complex nature of identity.

Making the film was anything but simple. "*Drink*," recalls Smith, "took two years of working after hours. I had always wanted to make films, but lacked the skill and knowledge of how to do it. As a matter of fact, I was learning very quickly since I had begun, and had to redo the first three quarters of it."

Another striking characteristic in *Drink* is Smith's use of morphing characters: it's a feature that will become the hallmark of his films. "The texture and the feel of morphing flesh appeals to me," says Smith. "It looks cool, it's symbolic, and it's surreal but expresses a powerful reality. The graphic quality of twisting material has inherent movement to it, and it lends itself to expressing a broad range of actions and emotions. My films all deal with inward struggle and the human psyche, and I think that this style expresses that well."

Encouraged by his success with *Drink* (which won over a dozen international awards), Smith followed his debut with *Delivery* (2003), the story of two friends (or brothers) sitting down watching television and eating popcorn. A courier drops off a mysterious box and the dark-haired man hits the light-haired guy and takes the box from him. As he lies on the ground, the light-haired man thinks of the years of abuse he has taken. He rises and kills his friend. He takes the box and opens it: it's empty.

For inspiration, Smith used a part of his own childhood. "My brother Dave used to grab me by my face, lift me off the ground, and throw me across the room. That's the first scene I animated and I constructed this story of rage and regret around this realistic action. I really wanted to kill the main character, which is exactly what I did in a graphic, cringing way. I wanted to make a tragedy cartoon. When this film premiered at Slamdance Film Festival, a woman approached me and said it was the worst cartoon she's ever seen."

Bullying brothers aside, *Delivery* is also addressing the larger issues of greed and violence in society. Every day we read stories of violence and murder motivated by seemingly mundane desires.

Using a simple, effective story with minimal characters, Smith creates a poignant analogy about the high price of violence and revenge. On a lighter level, Smith was also able to use animation to beat the shit out of his brother in a cartoon and effect some measure of personal satisfaction and revenge.

In *Handshake* (2004), Smith takes a unique and rather cynical look at relationships. A man and woman meet while waiting for a bus, shake hands and become literally stuck together. As they attempt to free themselves, they only become more entangled, eventually morphing into one another. Finally, the woman gets untangled and frees herself from the man. As she stands alone, unsure and somewhat sad, another man approaches, smiles and offers his hand.

Handshake is a downright nihilistic view of relationships, in a world where people do nothing but struggle to keep a grip on their identity. Smith's ending is a nice touch: no matter how suffocated and trapped we might have felt in a relationship, there's always another one waiting for us around the corner — short-term memory loss appears as we eagerly jump into the next handshake.

Smith's work was making strong impressions on the film circuit. Awards aside, he was also beginning to take on commissioned jobs to pay the bills. Aside from a number of commercials, Smith made his first music video, *Moving Along*, in 2004 for the UK band The Planets. While a part of the video recreates the morphing sequence from *Drink*, the bulk of the film, with its dark backgrounds and mysterious, masked characters, anticipates Smith's next and most recent film, *Puppet* (2006).

"Basically, the producer told me I could do whatever I wanted, so I made use of some random images and ideas I had from my sketchbook. The label was initially drawn to *Drink* and wanted that look. I gave them a similar idea, but with a darker, more foreboding, storyline. The idea of a sewn-up entity, carrying the world on its back, marching in sync with others, offers tons of symbolic meaning, perfect for the lyrics of the song."

Puppet continues to explore the themes of abuse and identity, this time through the use of an artist and his puppet. After the artist constructs a hand puppet, the puppet comes to life and begins assaulting its creator. Then with the help of another hand puppet, the duo turn the artist into their own puppet and force him to abuse himself and others.

"I always wanted to animate an antagonistic hand puppet smacking its owner," Smith says about *Puppet*. "The irony is intriguing and irresistible. I realized early on that this image was an analogy for the creative process and how we put our creations in a position where they can nearly destroy us. *Puppet* was the first film that I was actually happy with."

Smith has reason to be pleased with *Puppet*. The analogous approach is stronger than the earlier films and the narrative feels a bit more fleshed out. Still, Smith continues to struggle with the balance between personal and universal experiences. Too often in his work he seems scared of delving deeper. Analogy can be effective, but it also has a tendency to oversimplify complex issues. Smith's work often feels rushed conceptually, leaving the viewer wanting more.

Hard knocks? Call it tough love. Let's keep in perspective: this is a self-taught artist who has been making films for less than a decade. With each film, Smith has displayed growth and maturity as an artist. Smith's talent and potential is undeniable — as evidenced by the popularity of his films.

Smith is currently working on several projects. "I typically have three or four shorts happening at once, until one kind of rises to the surface, then I concentrate on that single idea. Since 2006, I've been heavily involved in crossing over to gallery exhibitions. Showing my films in new types of venues is a big interest of mine. My film *Masks* is actually a film/audio art installation that is written and engineered to screen within a gallery performance setting. I'm also working on some more 'public' pieces, using the city in a graffiti-type way, and incorporating that into an animated film."

Oh, and if there's any doubt about Smith's firmly established place as a respected voice in the indie animation scene, check out this nice piece of happenstance: a couple of years ago, Smith was asked to lecture at CalArts, the same school that rejected him twice.

"That was a small victory," admits Smith.

In animation, like life, you take the victories whenever you can get 'em.

Figure 7.1   Joanna Priestley

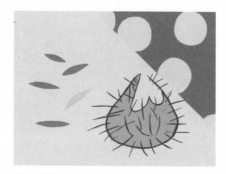

Figure 7.2   *Dew*

Figure 7.3   *Voices*

CHAPTER 7

Visions of Joanna Priestley

Portland animator Joanna Priestley is the undisputed queen of indie animation. While prominent women animators like Evelyn Lambart, Caroline Leaf and Suzan Pitt were making indie animation earlier, Priestley's films were unique in that she was the one of the few — maybe the only — female animators to use the medium in a direct, autobiographical manner. In films like *Voices*, *All My Relations*, *Grown Up* and the recent *Streetcar Named Perspire*, Priestley has tackled themes of personal fears, relationships, aging and menopause in a humorous and intimate manner. Priestley makes her films using an array of techniques including sand, puppet, cut-out and computer animation, collage and using materials such as rubber stamps, candy and index cards. The uniqueness, intimacy and power of Priestley's voice create a body of work (now upwards of 20 films) that is as comfortable, surprising and reliable as an old friend.

Priestley was seven years old when animation first appeared in her headlights. "For Christmas," recalls Priestley, "my parents gave me a tiny zoetrope that revolved on a beige, plastic turntable with a dozen drawing strips that fit inside. I was completely mesmerized by it." In high school she discovered the films of Canada's Norman McLaren, but it wasn't until she saw Chris Marker's *La Jetée* that Priestley finally had her animation epiphany. "Seeing *La*

Jetée detached me from gravity and threw me into the alternate universe of frame by frame filmmaking," says Priestley. "A professor at UC Berkeley showed the film in class and let me borrow the projector and 16 mm print. I immediately looked at it three more times. The first thing I wanted to see in Europe was the Museum of Natural History in Paris, one of the locations for the film. *La Jettée* led to producing multi-image shows (personal as well as commercial work) and that led to animation."

After high school, Priestley enrolled in the first animation class being offered at the Rhode Island School of Design. She then spent a year in Paris working as a printmaker before moving to the small town of Sisters, Oregon. "There were no movie theaters in Sisters nor in the three surrounding counties, an area half the size of Nova Scotia, so a friend and I started Strictly Cinema. We rented 16 mm prints and showed them at two high schools. People came in droves to the screenings. We started bringing in filmmakers, showing films outdoors in the park and having film festivals, including a big animation festival. I realized I could translate what I was doing in painting into filmmaking, so I went to the grocery store, bought a pack of index cards and started painting on them."

Priestley landed a job, through Strictly Cinema, as the film librarian and regional coordinator at the Northwest Film Center in Portland. Through this job she met a number of filmmakers and animators. "We brought in Gene Youngblood, author of *Expanded Cinema*, to be the juror for the Northwest Film and Video Festival," recalls Priestley. "He was on the faculty of CalArts and that led me to join their Experimental Animation, MFA program. I loved CalArts. The first computers arrived while I was there and I took the first computer animation class with faculty members Jules Engel, Myron Emery and Ed Emshwiller."

Although Priestley had already made three films, *Voices* (1985), Priestley's MFA thesis film at CalArts, was her first film to gain wider attention and clearly anticipate her future work. In this film Priestley appears before us on the screen and introduces herself as an animator. She tells us how she thinks about lots of things and, in a nice self-reflexive moment, she makes it very clear where she stands as an animator. As we encounter many references to animation history, Priestley talks about how she could simply make us laugh or could ask us to ponder heavy symbols. Instead, she offers herself, her "naked" face. This is not Disney or McLaren, but instead a personal diary of the artist's psychology. As she delves into her fears and worries, Priestley's face morphs into a variety of images (switching from drawn to rotoscope to cut-out animation) that articulate her ever-changing mindset. *Voices* is an engaging and modern animation that paints a picture, not of bunnies, mice and ducks or obtuse symbols, but of an everywoman whose thoughts about the world are readily identifiable and recognizable to most viewers.

Priestley's next film would establish a pattern of moving back and forth between the more narrative-driven personal films and nonlinear experimental and abstract works. This duality reflects Priestley's longtime appreciation of both ends of the animation spectrum: she loves Disney and Fleischer as much as McLaren.

She-Bop (1988) showed the more nonlinear, experimental side of Priestley's art. *She-Bop* was inspired not by the Cyndi Lauper song, but by a Carolyn Myers poem about the Great Goddess. "I heard her spontaneously perform it at a women's spirituality gathering in the woods," adds Priestley. Priestley met with Myers and recorded her reading the poem as the soundtrack for the film. Visually, the film is another marvel: Priestley creates a rich and colorful tapestry of images that complement the beat-inspired tones of Myers by using drawings, rotoscope and, for the first time, puppet animation. "I made a simple puppet with copper plates and lead wire and the set was made with Foamcore board," says Priestley.

Although Priestley is fiercely independent and, with the exception of sound, makes her films almost entirely on her own, she has collaborated with a few animators and artists over the years. The first of her collaborations was a humorous little project called *Candyjam* (1988).

In 1985, Priestley traveled to the Hiroshima International Animation Festival and met fellow Oregon animator Joan Gratz. "I was collecting beautiful Japanese candies and we talked about making a film with candy," recalls Priestley. "When we returned to Portland we asked filmmakers from several countries if they might be interested in contributing sequences of animated candy and everyone we asked said yes!" The result was a candy-coated collaboration with ten animators from four countries.

All My Relations (1990), the second of Priestley's four personal narratives, is an often hilarious and frank portrait of the ups and downs of relationships. Again using a mixture of techniques, Priestley has the drawn animation framed by various sculptured objects. "I added sculptural frames around the animation to create a new layer of content and visual relationships," explains Priestley. The soundtrack consists of the endless babble of a man and woman (voiced by improv comics Victoria and Scott Parker).

The voices are annoying, theatrical and absurd: the woman is neurotic, paranoid and insecure, and both spew a lot of nonsense. We're taken on a roller coaster ride of emotions as the woman's babble becomes increasingly hysterical. And, well, that's a pretty accurate depiction of much of the dialogue that does go on in relationships — so much emotional and physical energy spent in an absurd volley of nothings.

"I love collaborating with other creative people and I asked artists I admired to contribute frames. I knew from early on that I wanted to work with two improv comedians after I heard them create an entire soundtrack (in real time, including all the dialogue and sound effects) for a feature film screening at the Portland Art Museum."

In a beautiful moment of serendipity, the comic couple were in the process of getting a divorce while recording the soundtrack — that might explain the accuracy of their performance.

With *Pro and Con* (1992), Priestley (working again with Joan Gratz) returns to the personal narrative, but this time she examines a very different kind of relationship: that between correctional officers and prisoners. The film is certainly the most unusual in Priestley's body of work. This animation documentary is divided into two segments: pro and con. In the pro segment (directed by Priestley), Lt. Janice Inman, an African-American corrections officer, talks about her work and the importance of getting to know the inmates. The con segment (directed by Gratz) offers the perspective of inmate Jeff Green. Because Green was in solitary confinement, the animators had to communicate with him through his mother and later have an actor speak his words. Green talks about not trusting the officers, keeping to himself, his dreams for the future, and how desperately he misses women.

Pro and Con was made with a variety of techniques including clay painting, cel animation, paper drawing and puppet anima- tion. Meat was also used to symbolize the prisoner's feelings about how they are viewed and treated). Self-portraits drawn by inmates at the Oregon State Penitentiary were also used, as was animation of contraband weapons and crafts that had been seized from the inmates.

The end result is a striking piece of work that fuses not only various techniques, but animation and documentary to convey the complexities of a side of life few of us (we would hope . . .) can comprehend.

To make the film, Priestley and Gratz received funding from Portland's Percent for Art project. "A small percentage of the construction budget for a public building is dedicated to acquire art," says Priestley. "When a county jail was built, they decided to make a film with their Percent for Art funds. Joan Gratz and I were the only women and the only animators to apply."

After *Pro and Con* was completed, it was shown at the Oregon State Penitentiary. "It was a challenging experience," admits Priestley, "since the corrections officers left me alone in a class- room with 45 inmates. As I began speaking, half a dozen guys in the front row stood up and walked towards me, brushing against me as they passed by and out of the room. After the screening, eight men stayed late to talk to me about animation. They were very inspired and wanted to learn how to do it."

Almost ten years had passed since Priestley made *Voices*. She was now a recognized name in the international animation com- munity having won awards at a number of festivals. She also found herself hitting middle age and encountered a whole new range of emotions and thoughts. Sounds like a perfect scenario for a new Priestley film.

Grown Up — which uses a combination of pixilation, drawn and object animation — opens with the voice of a child saying, "You're a kid and then you turn 40." You might then expect a dour Dante-esque meditation on hitting middle age and finding yourself lost in the dark woods; instead, Priestley celebrates the joys of turning 40, of finally learning to live with yourself, of shutting out all the other voices and doing the things you want to do, the way you want to do them. Sure, there's death, lost relationships, physical changes, increase in hair (including a small mustache, apparently), but it's also the age when you finally get your shit together.

"I made *Grown Up* (1994) around the time I turned 40," says Priestley. "I finished the animation at the Djerassi artist's colony and was drawing ten hours a day, seven days a week. I later temporarily lost full use of my right arm because I was drawing so many hours a day. As with most limitations, it led to something interesting. Shooting the artwork for *Grown Up* was great fun because I incorporated animation of my hands with the artwork."

Grown Up would be the last of the personal narratives for another decade. The injury to her arm meant that she couldn't draw as much, so she decided to do more object animation. This led her towards a more abstract style of animation. For Priestley, it was essential that she keep growing and exploring as an artist. "I was profoundly influenced by the work of Norman McLaren when I was 15. I love the challenge of experimenting with new forms, new techniques, new subject matter, new color palettes and new genres. It's important that my work constantly evolves and I learn and grow with each new project. I crave the stimulation of new challenges and new discoveries."

Utopia Parkway (1997) was definitely a new direction. In this abstract piece, Priestley explores movement within contained spaces; animation occurs within bottles, frames, wooden boxes, cigar boxes. It's a fascinating work that touches on the idea that life is always in motion, even when it appears to be stagnant, echoing the words of the philosopher Heraclitus, who spoke of how the change of some things makes the existence of others possible. Rivers may remain the same, but the water is constantly changing: it is this constant change that makes the continued existence of the river possible. The various enclosures in *Utopia Parkway* remain unchanged on the surface, but within them change is constant.

The film was inspired by the boxes of Joseph Cornell, who lived on Utopia Parkway in Queens, New York, most of his life. "I was interested in an enclosure that creates a micro-universe," says Priestley. "I learned how to make latex molds from my new husband, Paul Harrod, and began experimenting with replacement animation of abstract sculptures that I placed in wood boxes and cigar boxes. It was also an excuse to ramble through junk and antique stores looking for boxes."

Priestley invited a number of local artists and animators to a dinner party and asked them to make small sculptures for the film. "I gave each person 18 to 20 Magic Sculpt (a two-part, epoxy-based, sculpture material) models of the same sculpture," says Priestley. "They had only one hour to fashion these into an animated sequence. Over the next four months I added additional sequences and sanded, painted and varnished all 122 sculptures. Each had a square peg in the back that registered on a smaller peg in a box. I also animated on index cards, but my injured arm limited the amount of time I could draw and paint. Most of the drawn animation was contained in squares and rectangles and I was happy with the quilt-like quality of the more complex sequences."

Surface Dive (2000) took abstract elements of *Utopia Parkway* even further: as water flows, assortments of strange colored sea objects appear, transform and leave. Again, the theme of change is at the heart of Priestley's films. Objects flow in and out; they come together and break apart; the only constant is the sound of the water and the continued, random existence of these strange, beautiful objects.

The film was inspired by a snorkeling experience Priestley had Mexico. "I was hitchhiking with a friend in the Yucatán and two guys picked us up. We made a stop in the middle of a vast, flat area. They grabbed diving masks and fins and asked us to follow them into the brush. We hiked half a mile and stopped at an oval pool of pale turquoise water. It was like swimming in a huge bowl of moss, woven with delicate, brown plant roots and filled with turquoise water and orange, pink and yellow fish. This was where a huge underground river met the sky and deep, black tunnels fell away on both sides. I suddenly realized the meaning of 'rapture of the deep': Divers go off into those tunnels and run out of air because it is so incredibly beautiful."

Priestley created 650 sculptures and registered them onto the back of pastel drawings in pencil. She shot the film on a homemade, multiplane animation stand with the sculptures on the top level, pieces of glass on the middle level and pastel drawings on the bottom level.

After collaborating with American animator Karen Aqua on a rather disappointing and old-fashioned experimental film (*Andaluz*, 2004), Priestley returned with another strong abstract film, *Dew Line* (2005).

Dew Line begins as a serene work full of warm and harmonious shapes and colors that evoke the calmness and wonder of nature. The peaceful tone is soon disrupted, however, by the rise of unyielding rectangular shapes that trigger death and destruction.

Priestley began the film in 2002 while she was teaching herself Flash animation and using the program to create abstract images. "I found it to be a friendly, intuitive program and I was delighted I could e-mail animation to friends. I bought a Wacom tablet and loved to scribble with it because of the way the pen slid around the smooth, plastic surface. I liked the 'Matisse look' of the solid color shapes of vector graphics. I remember that people thought this was a dreadful limitation, but it suited me fine because I was inspired by the color-field painters and by Matisse's cut-outs."

Becoming a medicinal herbalist influenced Priestley's rather grim ending. "I was increasingly concerned with global, environmental degradation. This seeped into *Dew Line*, leaving a slightly ominous resonance."

Streetcar Named Perspire (2007) marks a humorous return to the personal narrative. In what must be the first animation film ever made about menopause, a woman takes a roller coaster ride to demonstrate what it's like to go through this difficult, life-changing experience. "I was ambushed by the process at the beginning, because I knew nothing about it. I wanted to make an animated introduction to menopause so that others would not have to suffer the shock that I went through."

Priestley's latest film is called *Missed Aches* (2009). "I had been to the Wordstock literary festival and heard slam poet Taylor Mali do a poem about proofreading. The elderly lady next to me, wearing a grey, knit suit, laughed so hard she fell off her chair. I spent months trying to reach him and my efforts led to a wonderful collaboration. *Missed Aches* is also made with Flash."

Over 20 years have passed since Priestley first began making independent animation shorts; the animation scene has changed dramatically over this time. "When I began making films, there were hundreds of people doing independent animated short films. It was considered to be [a] very arcane, marginal activity that did not lead to a 'real' job. Now there are tens of thousands of indie animation filmmakers making wonderful short films and features and their efforts can lead to an 'A-list' job in the commercial world."

As diverse as Priestley's body of work has been, the one constant is a search for balance: throughout the personal narratives, she searches for a sense of personal balance, and in the experimental and abstract works, Priestley seeks it on an environment level. Ultimately Priestley's sense of balance and harmony is derived from making films. "I make films because I enjoy the process. I love going to my cozy studio every day and exploring with color, line, texture, and sound. Animation is a way to create 'life' and new movement and to explore new worlds. Life is good!"

Figure 8.1   Barry Purves

Figure 8.2   *Gilbert and Sullivan*

Figure 8.3   *Achilles*

CHAPTER 8

Barry Purves

The Puppetmaster

Puppets and dolls have always freaked me out. When I was quite
young, I encountered a Raggedy Ann doll on the dark streets of
Toronto and that creepy dead/alive face scared the shit out of
me. Puppets and dolls seem to live on that border between life
and death, between the inanimate and animate. I'm obviously
not alone in my fear: *Child's Play* and *Puppetmaster* were popular
horror films about evil dolls and puppets. A few days ago I heard
an old radio show called *Dimension X* — this particular episode
dealt with aliens who posed as children's dolls in an attempt to
takeover the world. I figure that the fear of puppets and dolls is
somehow linked to our fear of death. I saw my first dead person
a few years ago and, well, it creeped me out — that sensation of
dead/alive returned.

Now, what does all this have to do with Barry Purves? Well,
the British animator is among the most acclaimed puppet animators in the world. His passion, care and attention to detail and
movements have produced eerily realistic puppets that convey
such powerful emotions that the viewer often forgets that they're
watching animation.

Purves's acclaimed short films (including the 1993 Oscar nominee *Screenplay*) are influenced by Greek mythology, literature,

opera, and theater. Through his human-like puppets, Purves explores issues of sexuality, identity, mortality and passion, while attempting to understand the complexities of human relationships and emotions.

Born in Woodbridge, Suffolk, England, Purves had what he called a "pretty creative childhood." His parents took him to the theater and movies, he participated in plays at school, and throughout his teens was involved with a variety of productions under the charge of British composer, Benjamin Britten.

After studying drama and Greek civilization at Manchester University in the mid-1970s, Purves worked in theaters for a couple of years, primarily as a stage manager. While working at a theater in Scotland, Purves met Mark Hall who, with partner Brian Cosgrove, was running an animation studio called Cosgrove Hall Films. Purves was frustrated with the lack of creativity in his theater work, and was given a job audition by Hall. Purves had no puppet animation experience but had done some drawn and cut-out animation. Hall was impressed with Purves work and hired him.

Purves worked for Cosgrove Hall for nine years and during that time he worked on a number of TV productions, including *Chorlton and the Wheelies* and *The Wind and the Willows*. "My first solid nine years there," says Purves, "were the most exciting. When Mark and Brian were still there, it was very much hands-on, creating a wonderful, friendly, experimental and encouraging atmosphere. We all seemed to be inventing it as we went along. I loved Cosgrove Hall's integrity about standards, storytelling, and character.

In 1986, Purves "was getting itchy feet to do something

different," so he left Cosgrove Hall and started working at Aardman Animations studio in Bristol. He worked on a pilot for a proposed children's series, *Hamilton Mattress* (he'd eventually make this film in 2001), and animated a number of commercials.

While at Aardman, Purves finally had a chance, in 1989, to make his own film: the British TV station Channel 4 commissioned the studio to make a lip-sync series. They wanted films that played with language (one of the films, Nick Park's *Creature Comforts* would win an Oscar for Best Animated Short Film) and so Purves chose William Shakespeare as his subject, but with a bit of a twist. "I chose to use visual and body language as my theme," recalls Purves. "I'm not particularly keen on facial expressions (as long as the puppets have good eyes). I'd rather concentrate on elegant body movement that armatured puppets allow so well. *Next* became a film about trying to use the body/puppet in as many different ways as possible."

In this dizzyingly fast-paced and clever film, Shakespeare appears on stage for an apparent audition. Without words, he frantically performs parts from all of his plays (no, I didn't count, but Purves assures me every play is represented). The character's movements are as graceful and fluid as a dancer's. The face is so realistic that you would swear you are observing a real human head. Of course, you are left with the questions, why is Shakespeare auditioning? Who is he auditioning for? After the performance, Shakespeare eagerly awaits his judgement; after deliberating, the critic (who is actually Saint Peter, Heaven's doorman) laughs and says, "What fools these mortals be." Shakespeare's audition, it seems, has actually been him living his life — and apparently he has failed.

Having Shakespeare perform his plays for Saint Peter is a hilarious idea, but to then force him to pantomime his plays is a sweet dash of bastardly brilliance. Even more incredible is that these two ideas were not in Purves's original plans and only came about because of financial constraints. "*Next* started out as wanting to be something about the Shakespeare plays. I had wanted a sizeable cast of characters, but the budget only allowed for one decent puppet, and the emphasis then shifted towards Shakespeare himself." At one point, Purves was even considering having a cast of famous actors each read a line of Shakespeare's, but the high cost of copyright put that idea to death. Who says having a small budget is a bad thing?

Purves worked at Aardman for a couple more years before leaving in 1992 to start his own production company, Bare Boards Productions, with Glenn Holberton. "It was probably one of the two big career mistakes I made by not staying at Aardman, though I left when there was a bit of a quiet period. If I had stayed I might not have made my own films, but I would certainly have worked on some exciting projects." His other mistake? Not accepting to work on Gollum for Peter Jackson's *The Lord of the Rings* film trilogy.

One of Purves's first projects for Bare Boards was *Screenplay* (1992), presented as a Japanese Kabuki play. A revolving set sits in the middle of the frame. A narrator enters the scene and tells a tale of forbidden lovers who go against their families to be together. Throughout the tale, moving screens trigger the change in scenes but the camera remains stationary, giving the viewer the feeling of being in the audience at a live performance.

Just when it looks like the story has ended happily, a hideous, masked creature breaks through the screen, slices the narrator's head off and opens another screen to hunt down the lovers — blood and guts flood the screen. The creature kills the man before being killed by the woman and then, alone, the woman takes her own life. In an instant, Purves's stylish, sexy (the lovers appear nude and make love — yes, the male puppet even has a penis with pubes) and romantic tale turns into a Quentin Tarantino-style bloodbath. As the bloodshed begins, switching the perspective of the tale, Purves also switches the audience's perspective. The camera comes alive and brings the viewer right smack into the action. Our distant, objective distance is shattered, as we become participants in the carnage. After everyone is suitably dead, the camera pulls back to reveal another screen, further revealed as part of a film set, and the camera then pulls back again to reveal a marked-up script in a binder; finally, we see a hand mark a check on the script and close the binder. The filmstrip flickers into darkness.

With *Screenplay*, Purves was taking the concept of visual language to another level. "*Screenplay*," he says, "became about using as many different forms of visual language as possible, from the coded language of sign language, to the cultural language of Kabuki."

As for the stationary camera, Purves says, "the long sustained shot not only reflects a theatrical storytelling, but it is also about having an adrenalin rush whilst filming. I like the challenge of such long sustained shots. I don't really enjoy very short shots where the performance is created through editing. I want to see the performance."

In the early 1990s, the BBC commissioned a series of animation films that would be based on operas. The intent was to introduce opera to a more general audience (and perhaps show some folks that animation can indeed be used for mature purposes?). Although the series was largely a failure — most of the films were poorly adapted and animated — Purves's animation of Verdi's *Rigoletto* was, by far, the standout.

Verdi's sinister tale of debauchery, murder and a doomed father and daughter is a perfect fit for Purves's sensibilities. The depth and detail of Purves's sets and character design captures the dirty, vile decadence of this world and its people. Purves's camera work, shifting between startling zooms, graceful Ophuls-style tracking shots and unsettling tilted "Batman" shots suggests a suffocating, oppressive hell.

As rich as the film is, at times it begins to feel that technique and craft are overshadowing the animation and story. Purves admits that if he had a chance to remake *Rigoletto* it would be "less literal." Yet, the film remains one of Purves's most popular films. "*Rigoletto* still gets a huge response," adds Purves, "and seems to move people. It is certainly a rich lavish film, and I enjoyed working with such a dark storyline and troubled characters."

In his next film, *Achilles* (1995), Purves turned to Greek mythology for inspiration. In what has to be the first gay male soft porn puppet film, Purves's film looks at the repressed passions Achilles (the great warrior of Homer's war epic, *The Illiad*) carries for Patroclus.

In Greek mythology, the handsome Achilles was the hero of the Trojan (serendipitous pun) War. In *The Illiad*, Patroclus and Achilles have a deep, intimate relationship, and Achilles becomes distraught when Patroclus is killed by Hector, the Trojan leader.

Achilles goes apeshit and rescinds his vow not to fight in the war, going on a rampage that ends with the murder of Hector; Paris, Hector's brother, subsequently kills Achilles.

Purves's *Achilles* largely focuses on Achilles' struggle in accepting his love for Patroclus. Achilles rejects Patroclus's obvious advances — likely out of fear of what his men will think — but later, as he struggles with his feelings, he loses himself in a soft porn fantasy where all his desires and passions come to life in a tender, sensual love scene with Patroclus.

Once again, Purves used no dialogue (except for Derek Jacobi's narration) and relied solely on body language to express the anguished desires of Achilles. As with *Screenplay*, Purves placed a stage at the centre of the frame (this time a crumbling circular stone) for the "actors" to perform their play. This strategy allowed Purves to move away from the usually abundant sets of *Rigoletto*, so that the viewer can focus more on the characters and animation. To further separate the two main characters from the rest of the cast, Purves gave them the look of cracked, white statues.

Purves remains pleased with *Achilles*. "*Achilles*," he says, "is the film I think I got right. It started out as a film about Orpheus and Eurydice, and related characters who looked where they should not have looked. I wanted to work with a Greek chorus, again using the idea of body language extended to a large group, having large choreographed movement."

When time constraints limited the amount of work Purves could do, he turned his focus to the intimate relationship between Achilles and Patroclus. "This was another challenge for me. I wanted to make an erotic film using puppets, with sensual scenes that were taken seriously. I was trying to push what puppets can do."

In the mid-1990s, Purves had a brief taste of Hollywood when he was hired as the animation director for Tim Burton's 1950s-inspired sci-fi film *Mars Attacks!* Elaborate sets were built under Purves's direction. "We spent months working on bizarre little Martian gestures and ways of moving," Purves recalled to Wendy Jackson of *Animation World Magazine* in 1997. "The animation tests were looking good and suitably creepy." Then Warner Bros. decided that it made more sense to use computers. In a flash, nine months of painstaking puppet work was tossed and Purves was out of a job.

"*Mars Attacks!*" adds Purves, "happened at the time when technology was exploding forth, and seemed, I guess, the more economical way to go, and the computer graphics did things we certainly could not have done. Of course I was sad not to have been involved with the CG Martians, (what fantastic creations they were — when I was involved I was trying to model them on Norma Desmond) and maybe I simply wasn't good enough, but I don't think that the film was the death of stop-motion as most people feared it might be. I think it was more the start of CG showing what it does best, and thus leading stop-motion to show what it does best."

Purves returned home and began work on a new film. In the vein of *Next, Gilbert and Sullivan: The Very Models* (1998) features Gilbert and Sullivan starring in an opera about the period following their introduction to each other by Richard D'Oyly Carte (the third character in the film). As D'Oyly Carte sits on his bed, Gilbert and Sullivan play an assortment of male and female roles from their operas. The film has the feel of a dream: Gilbert and Sullivan are of a ghostly pale (reminiscent of Achilles and Petrolus). The two men spend most of their time squabbling like a pair of children as D'Oyly Carte tries to keep them together with promises of fame and fortune. The film follows the relationship of the three men through to the deaths of Gilbert and Sullivan, after which D'Oyly Carte dances and falls back on his bed exhausted. The dream (or nightmare) is over.

Gilbert and Sullivan was first and foremost a tribute to two artists Purves had loved since an early age, "I love the relationship between Gilbert and Sullivan. To call them friends would be generous, but in spite of their coldness, they did work together brilliantly producing such masterpieces. The glue that kept these two men together was D'Oyly Carte and I was pleased to make a film that acknowledges his contributions to these works."

Purves was also interested in the conflict between commercial and personal work: swayed by their fame and fortune, the duo was content to keep churning out popular commercial fare rather than explore more risky and personal works. By this time in his career, Purves knew firsthand about these struggles. He had the aborted experience with *Mars Attacks!* and it was becoming clear that Channel 4 (who almost single-handedly gave birth to and maintained a thriving independent animation scene in England in the 1980s and 1990s) would no longer be funding short-form animation. In fact, *Gilbert and Sullivan* remains Purves's last independent film.

As successful and acclaimed as Purves's films have been, there have been people in the animation world who have criticized his work for being too theatrical. "I find it odd that my work is criticized for being theatrical," says Purves. "I really don't feel comfortable seeing animation in a bubble isolated from the other arts. Like opera, ballet, and theater it's a medium that revels in its very falseness. It works best when we are aware of the medium. As we watch a dancer making beautiful shapes and movements, we are also aware of how she is pushing her body over perceived limits and defying gravity, so I think animation works well when we see the technique. I really am so allergic to the literal, and don't see the point. I don't see the point of animation when we try to copy real life."

Ironically, some have criticized Purves's work as being too realistic. Why spend so much time creating realistic-looking puppets when you could just work with humans?

"I come on very defensive when I hear this criticism," admits Purves. "My films are not in any way realistic. Two Greek statues having sex in a spotlight on a stone arena watched by a chorus of masked figures is hardly realistic, *but* it is credible and that is the difference. The movement of the puppets of *Achilles* is hardly realistic but borders on choreography. The movement in my films may be smooth, sometimes at least, and that's what people may confuse with realism, but realistic it is not, no more than a dancer or an actor on a stage. Or maybe it is the assumption that because I use human-based characters then they are realistic, but actually Shakespeare is not very realistic, proportionally certainly, and Gilbert and Sullivan are total caricature."

Purves has only made one more film since *Gilbert and Sullivan*: the children's TV special *Hamilton Mattress*, about an aardvark drummer who hopes to make it the big city. Purves did not write the special, and while it seems miles away from his personal films, he was pleased with the experience. "*Hamilton Mattress* was practically the last of the big TV specials to be commissioned before the broadcasters lost enthusiasm for animation, and it was an absolute joy to work with a great budget, and a fantastically creative crew."

A common theme that runs through Purves's films is a sense of failure and disappointment: none of his characters gets what they desire. These days, Purves finds himself in a similar situation. "I fear I am actually no nearer to getting a film made than I was a few years ago. It does scare me that I'm going to spend the rest of my career talking about animation rather than being a practitioner." Without the funding necessary to make more independent shorts, he has taken on television work like *Rupert the Bear* and has designed a Christmas show. "Funders seem happier to give what limited funds there are to first-time animators — and why not, as what a great break that is, but it is sad to see something for which there clearly is an appreciative audience not being exploited. I do worry what will happen to all these animators we are so busy training."

You would think that being internationally renowned as one of the masters of animation, Purves would have no trouble finding funding. "Isn't that odd? I really don't see myself as being terribly successful, as I have certainly not got to the stage where my name or my work might give a script any credibility. And certainly financially my career definitely can't be viewed as successful. Thirty years of filmmaking doesn't open any special funding doors. But I do recognize that I've done a decent variety of work and some of it still holds up well today, and that most importantly to me, most of it has been quite unique and hopefully, quite classy and with a certain integrity."

Samuel Beckett's line from *The Unnamable*, "I can't go on, I'll go on," might best describe indie animators like Purves: no matter how dour things become, they somehow find a way to keep on. This almost belligerent determination emanates from a deep-seeded passion that animators absorb from their art. "The joy of touching a puppet will never diminish," says Purves. "I'm thrilled to have had the chance to make films that possibly were different. I've been told again and again that I am too idiosyncratic. I sort of take that as a compliment."

Figure 9.1   Michaela Pavlátová

Figure 9.2   *Az na veky*

Figure 9.3   *Karneval*

CHAPTER 9

Michaela Pavlátová's Carnal Carnival

Throughout her career, Oscar-nominated Czech animator Michaela Pavlátová has explored relationships — specifically how language, boredom, sex and death foul up marriages. Pavlátová's approach is blunt and occasionally ferocious. She is not interested in singular romantic definitions of marriage and love; for Pavlátová, the relations between men and women are infinitely complex emotional and physical processes of joy, repetition, anger, hostility, abuse, intimacy and loneliness.

Pavlátová attributes her obsession with relationships to "my lack of fantasy. It is much easier for me to be inspired by watching what is going on around me, or what happens in my own life. I know how it tastes to betray as well as to be betrayed. To love and being loved as well as the opposite. Somehow, male/female relationships are still the most interesting theme for me. It embraces everything, can be funny, ridiculous, dramatic, exciting, anything, you can get a comedy as well as a tragedy."

Although she doesn't really remember how she became interested in animation, Pavlátová does remember when she was first introduced to film. When a Japanese animator visited her fifth-grade class in Prague, he gave the young Czech a Super 8 camera and a few rolls of film. "I discovered," remembers Pavlátová, "the pleasure of creating something just by myself, at home, creating a film."

After high school, Pavlátová wanted to attend the Academy of Applied Arts and found that the only department she could get into was animation.

Pavlátová was fortunate to graduate from school before the dissolution of Czechoslovakia into the Czech Republic and Slovakia. The state studio Krátký Film was still receiving a budget from the state and they had a minimum number of animation films that they needed to produce each year. "I did three animated short movies at the beginning which were like a presentation where I could show that I was able to do something," says Pavlátová. "If I were in the situation of the students who are finishing school right now, I am not sure I would have enough will to continue. There is so much work but you don't have money for it and it is not shown anywhere."

Pavlátová was indeed fortunate. While her first two films, *An Etude from the Album* (1987) and *The Crossword Puzzle* (1989) address themes that would occupy Pavlátová throughout her animation career (language and the relationship between men and women), neither film is particularly memorable, nor do they show signs of an acclaimed animator in the making.

Initially Pavlátová wanted to make a trilogy about marriage at different stages of life. *Etude* looks at a tired old couple, while *Crossword Puzzle* playfully pokes fun at a poor sex-hungry woman and her puzzle-obsessed husband. While there are hints of Pavlátová's distinct drawing style, the animation and stories are too simplistic, reflecting an artist too young to take on such complex issues. Pavlátová agrees and says that *Crossword Puzzle* is

"my least favourite film. About half way through the film I realized that I didn't like the design or the story, but somehow I had
to finish it." With *Etude*, Pavlátová chalks it up to inexperience:
"I did not know anything about film directing, about animation.
I just tried my best. Pretty naive film, I think."

Third time's a charm: in 1991, Pavlátová made her mark on
the international animation stage with the brilliant *Words, Words,
Words.* People in a crowded bar talk only with visual bubbles and
objects. The clientele include a loner woman, a dull couple and
gossipy ladies; there are young and old, and even a drinking dog.
People are happy, sullen, drunk, horny, dying and angry. In the
final scene, the once lonely woman, who has lived through the
ups and downs of an entire relationship in the bar, recognizes
her selfishness, completes the couple's puzzle (which hangs in the
air above her) and races off to her lover. The film then ends as
it begins — with the waiter alone, surrounded by empty tables.

Words, Words, Words is a nifty piece of caricature and insight
that takes us through the roller coaster ride of emotions that are
human relationships. It's a situation most of us have been in, as
observer or observed. We have all sat in a café or on a bus or patio
people-watching, catching snippets of conversations and gestures
that we then construct into a portrait of the observed. In these
moments, we see the spectrum of humanity — a wonderful,
painful kaleidoscope of social interaction.

"In the beginning," says Pavlátová, "I had many drawings of
people 'talking' with bubbles, and then I spent a long time trying to figure out how to put together these individual ideas. In
terms of story structure, it's probably my best-constructed film.
I remember that the last day, after the final mix, I started to cry

because I was so disappointed with the film. But it was my 'most successful' one and brought me many surprising awards."

The film won a slew of awards including Grand Prizes in Spain, Montreal, Brazil, Turkey and Germany. Pavlátová also received a 1993 Oscar nomination and became an instant star on the international animation circuit.

Following her success with *Words, Words, Words*, Pavlátová was offered a chance to make a segment for Dutch animator Paul Driessen's film, *Uncles and Aunts*. "It is so long ago," says Pavlátová, "that I cannot remember how it begun. I met Paul Driessen in Varna in 1989. We became friends and he offered me a part of *Uncles and Aunts*. He said that he didn't want to make it by himself. For me it was a great chance to get his name in the credits and make me look more 'famous.' I began to work on it in Holland, finished the animation back in Prague, then sent it to Paul, so the sound and all post-production was work of him and producer Nico Crama."

Uncles and Aunts is a strange and inconsistent series of snapshot gags about parents, cousins, aunts and uncles: a mother isn't thrilled with her sex-starved husband, an Aunt makes pancakes to toss at her husband, a cousin spends so much time reading that his head physically expands, an Uncle makes his wife's breasts grow with a remote. Some of the snapshots are funny and Pavlátová's drawings are full of energy and wit, but overall the episodes don't really generate more than a shrug.

Repete (1995) is a return to peak form for Pavlátová. Beautifully conceived, animated and drawn (using paint and pencils), *Repete* observes the lives of three couples. The starting point is a man taking his dog for a walk; different people go by him. We are then taken into three scenes: in the first, a woman is feeding her husband; in the second, a woman frees a suicidal man then rejects him; in the third, a man and woman are about to make love, but a ringing phone interrupts them. These three scenes play out again and again until the walking dog stops, causing all the scenes to shift slightly. Taken out of their daily rhythms, the perspectives of the three couples change. Released from their tedious cycle, the three scenes collide and form new relationships. Fresh possibilities are discovered — until they too drift into mundane cycles.

Repete is a perfect display of Pavlátová's complex attitude towards relationships. She does not make things easy for her audience: there are no clear-cut answers. Pavlátová refuses to pander to polarized perspectives that pinpoint relationships as good or bad; relationships can be profound, absurd, tedious and heartbreaking — this is the reality.

"I was married for couple of years at that time," says Pavlátová. "It did not work as I imagined. This film was my attempt to make a film just by myself, without help of anyone else, just to draw everything at home and then to bring the box of papers to the studio — (that's why the film does not have any backgrounds.)"

Repete was an international success, winning Grand Prizes in Uruguay and Japan, along with a prestigious Golden Bear award at the Berlin International Film Festival.

BBC Bristol had a regular animation program, and to introduce the animators to their viewers, the BBC commissioned various animators to make very short self-portrait films.

Pavlátová's contribution was *This Could Be Me* (1996). In a quiet, sexy and playful voice, Pavlátová narrates this primarily live-action self-portrait, taking the viewer through the streets of

Prague to her studio/apartment. Inside, she shows us things that are important to her: pictures, art, tools and books. Little snippets of paper animation appear in the background as Pavlátová talks about being a child, growing up and loathing having to make decisions for herself. Finally, she talks about the importance of her relationships and her interest in the relations between men and women; she admits that she loves to observe people.

For a modest film, *This Could Be Me* offers some insight into Pavlátová's life and influences. Pavlátová sprinkles the film with humor and bits of absurdity, showing us that as much as she is passionate about relationships and friends and family, she isn't a person that takes life all that seriously.

"This is my favourite one," Pavlátová says of the film. "I thought that this could be a good chance to try to make something bit different and addressed a friend of mine, documentary film-maker Pavel Koutecký. We just improvised, something which was absolutely new for me. I drew various animations which we shot in my studio at that time and in the streets of Prague. We improvised also at the editing room, it was a first time that I enjoyed the feeling of spontaneous creating."

Pavlátová uses some of the drawings and experiments from *This Could Be Me*, for her next film, *Forever and Ever* (1998). Combining live-action footage with a variety of animation techniques (drawn, paint-on-glass, index cards, cut-out), Pavlátová takes a cynical stab at marriage. The live-action scenes show the happy atmosphere of a wedding: kids play, couples smile and dance, everything is wonderful, hope and possibility swarms the atmosphere. But what happens after the wedding? The animation segments undermine the joy of the wedding by exploring the frustration (a child interrupting his parents' attempt to make love), imbalance (a husband as a helpless little boy), and loneliness (the couple unable to communicate with each other) of marriage.

For all its biting wit and insight, *Forever and Ever* comes off as a bitter, reactionary film. Pavlátová cannot hide her own apparent bitterness towards relationships, and ends up spouting the type of polarized views she deftly managed to avoid in previous films.

"Yes, it is the mistake of the movie," admits Pavlátová. "It was not meant to be so hostile. I wanted to say that living with someone can be nice or not so nice, we expect that our life will not repeat the mistakes of couples around us, but it can happen this way — or another way."

In 2000, Pavlátová followed her boyfriend to San Francisco. It was good timing on the animation front because the internet boom was taking off. In San Francisco, Pavlátová met John Hayes, one of the owners of Wild Brain Animation Studios. At the time, Wild Brain was producing highly innovative Flash animation series for the internet. Hayes offered Pavlátová a chance to make her own series, and she would be given total freedom.

Before tackling the online series, Pavlátová made the Flash film *Taily Tales* (2001), a goofy short about a cat's erotic relationship with her tail. "*Taily Tales*," says Pavlátová, "was originally just my exercise in Flash. I was learning it from tutorial and it just somehow finished as a small film."

She settled on a series called *Graveyard*, a collection of 13 short Flash animation pieces about gruesome and ridiculous death scenes involving couples, toddlers, lovers, young women, etc. . . . "I was inspired by *The Darwin Awards*," says Pavlátová, "a book collecting ridiculous causes of death from local newspapers."

While both the design and the concept are more straightforward and playful than in Pavlátová's other work, *Graveyard* possesses her stinging and blunt black humor.

Unfortunately, *Graveyard* never played online; just as she finished the thirteen parts, the internet animation scene wilted and died. Pavlátová stayed at Wild Brain, made two commercials and submitted a number of series pitches (including one for a proposed children's series named *Naptime*). Then Pavlátová received an offer to direct a live-action feature film in Prague so she packed her bags, said farewell to San Fran and headed home.

While working on the feature film, *Faithless Games* (2003), Pavlátová continued to make small animation Flash films on the side. Pavlátová calls *Laila* (2003–6) "my secret pleasure. Like if you are a musician, sometimes you just want to play your instrument, as an animator, sometimes you just feel a big need to animate."

Using the format of a diary, *Laila* takes us inside the mind of a woman as she writes about her jumbled, paranoid thoughts about mortality, sex, dead animals and, naturally, relationships. "Inspiration for *Laila*," says Pavlátová, "came from various experiences from my life. Originally I wanted to make something like an animated diary, every week or so, to react to things happening around me. But then I had less time and also, there was not any right frustration to push me to make another *Laila*. If I am happy and satisfied, there can't be any new Lailas."

In 2004, Pavlátová was invited to teach animation at Harvard University. Being exposed daily to enthusiastic and ambitious animation students excited Pavlátová and inspired her to get home and make another film.

For years she had wanted to make an erotic film, but never found a structure that worked. "Everything I did was too pathetic, too serious. Everything turned out to be ridiculous. Then I have got the inspiration from the incorrigible, mischievous drawings of my friend, illustrator Vratislav Hlavatý. I wanted to enjoy a long process of work on it, so I decided to structure the film in two episodes, where each one examines different aspects of sexuality and each one is drawn in a different style."

The Carnival of Animals (2006), Pavlátová's "animated erotic-musical fantasy," is taken from the famous musical suite by French composer Saint-Saëns. Parts of the suite have been heard in a number of Warner Bros. cartoons and the finale was also used in Disney's *Fantasia 2000*. The suite's light and jaunty rhythms — with a dash of satire — fit Pavlátová's goofy sexcapade as comfortably as a good "meat dance".

With the feel of an erotic dream, a stream of sexual imagery briskly moves in and out of focus. Young girls lament their small titties and shave their armpits in anticipation of boys. The two sexes eye each other with suspicion from afar until a girl bravely grabs a boy's penis — and away we go into a dazzling segment of playing cards with tits and penises on them flickering about to the frolicking pulse of Saint-Saëns' "Pianists." We then step inside the dreams of two sleeping lovers (revealing their many cloaked and crazy desires), before checking out a guy's first awkward sex experience — represented as a tiny man trying to mount a giant woman. In the gang-bang finale, everyone cums together: animals, men, and women.

Rabbits perform a circle jerk on each other's ears, animals chase women, men mount animals. It's one big smorgasbord of unleashed sexual desire that climaxes in the mother of all orgasms.

The Carnival of Animals is one of Pavlátová's most accomplished and joyous films. This isn't a gushy romantic piece about nice men and women being in love and hugging each other; it's an all-out celebration of sex and desire in all its bizarre, ugly, awkward, frivolous and violent forms. Pavlátová takes us to places real, imagined and dreamed: a world that only animation could show us.

"It is a bit risky theme," says Pavlátová about *Carnivals*, "because everyone's line between what is still erotic and what is already vulgar is different. Also, it can be very pathetic and turn ridiculous if we want to show sex very seriously. I found that the only way to speak about it is by making fun of it. (Probably something very similar with speaking about death.)"

Frustrated by small audiences and limited funding, Pavlátová finds herself struggling to find her passion for animation today. "Oh! You touched the problem! I miss the motivation to make another short animated film. It may change and I hope it will. Animation shorts are something that no one needs and mankind can survive without it. We are just like crazy people who damage their eyes and vision with animating but somehow we like doing it."

Sounds like an ideal relationship.

Figure 10.1   Théodore Ushev

Figure 10.2   *Sou*

Figure 10.3   *Vertical*

CHAPTER 10

Théodore Ushev

Man Called Aerodynamics

Bulgarian-born Montreal animator, Théodore Ushev is an animation anomaly. His films, steeped in old-world ideas, are filtered through modern technologies that enable him to convey his thoughts fast. Animators have a tendency to take anywhere from five to ten years to make their precious films. This makes it difficult to create art that speaks to the moment and that has, arguably, always been one of the drawbacks of animation: it often lacks urgency and immediacy. An academic twit once called animation the "ceramics of cinema". Harsh words that I don't subscribe to, but I can understand why people think this way. Animators make precious, polished little films that don't seem to have much impact on the world. Théodore's handling of animation, however, is raw, rough and chaotic; there's nothing polished, pristine or precious about his approach. His best films (*Tower Bawher* and *Drux Flux*) were made, incredibly, in just three weeks. Ushev can't help it — he has a burning passion and desire to communicate. His work, which hardly ever looks the same, is a quest to uncover chaos of his moment — and ours. Ironically, unlike so many indie animators, Ushev always wanted to be an animator, but animation didn't always want him.

Ushev, the son of a journalist and an abstract painter, developed an interest in animation in high school and even made a short film before graduating. Ushev wanted to study animation at the National Academy of Fine Arts in Sofia; however, the academy had an abundance of animation students and so, for a couple of years, was not accepting new applicants. Instead, Ushev did his mandatory two-year military service while he worked as a mural artist. After doing his time, he returned to the Academy and enrolled in graphic and poster design.

During his studies (he graduated with his master's degree in 1995), Ushev did various freelance jobs on the side. One of his designs won a CorelDRAW design contest for computer graphic and design. "This was the golden age of Corel Corporation," says Ushev. "They invited me to Ottawa for the award ceremony and covered all my expenses." Ushev won two more Corel awards and during the third visit, an immigration officer asked him if he wanted a permanent residence visa. "I said, why not," recalls Ushev. I packed my bag and came to visit some animation friends in Montreal. It was the golden age of multimedia in Montreal. I found a job as an art director in one of those 'new' dot-com companies, where they where giving free bagels and bananas to the staff, and recreational massages in the lunchtime. It was a pretty good time to be a designer."

Ushev's work often required him to design interactive and multimedia websites for fashion companies in Montreal. This meant learning the new Adobe Flash software. Discovering this software also led Ushev back to animation. Over time he became dissatisfied with his jobs, so to amuse himself he started making a short Flash animation film. "They gave me the freedom to do what I want," recalls Ushev. "I didn't care too much about the results. They didn't cost much to do and I did them in my free time."

During this period, Ushev made a number of interesting Flash films, including *Dissociation* (2001), about a man stuck in a dead-end office job and dreams of love and freedom; *Early in Fall, Late in Winter* (2002), about the life and death of a romance; *Walking On By* (2003), where a stick figure walks along a line and encounters all sorts of people and obstacles until he literally reaches the end of the line; *Well-Tempered Heads* (2003), featuring music by Bach where the piano keys turn into a rotating series of wood-carved heads that become increasingly splintered and pained.

Ushev's early films lack the sophistication and depth of his later work, but they are remarkable for a couple of reasons. First, while he does deal with potentially cliché subjects like doomed love, existentialism and the evils of power, Ushev manages to do so in a somewhat lighthearted manner. His characters take their pain: they absorb it and move on. There's no hysterics or wrist slitting. Pain and disappointment are natural parts of life. Secondly, these films were made in the early days of Flash animation. With few exceptions (for example the online work of San Francisco's Wild Brain Animation Studio and that of Canadian animator Ed Beals), Flash works of that period were flaccid and juvenile, littered with idiotic gags and goofy characters that would barely amuse a brain-damaged ten-year-old. Ushev's inspired and deeply personal and mature narratives were akin to finding water in a desert.

Animation became more than a hobby for Ushev when *Early Fall, Late Winter* was accepted into competition in 2003 by the

Annecy, France, and Ottawa, Canada, festivals — the two largest animation festivals. At this time, producer Michael Fukushima at the legendary National Film Board of Canada (NFB) saw Ushev's work and suggested he propose a film to the studio. Ushev's proposal for a film based on a Franz Kafka story called *The Man Who Waited* was rejected, but he was offered a chance to make a film for the NFB's Cineweb series, which was aimed at encouraging emerging animators to make low-budget internet films.

Ushev's contribution to Cineweb was the film *Vertical* (2003), a simple but effective piece about the fall of society. Graphically influenced by Polish animator Jan Lenica's push-pin graphics, *Vertical* shows men, birds, bottles, words and sanity sliding down into a perpetual cycle of ruin. The Nino Rota-influenced soundtrack that seems pinched from a merry-go-round captures the absurdity of the characters as they struggle to keep from falling. Finally, the last shot ends where it began. There is no end to the fall, the world just keeps going round and round as people continue to make the same irrational and selfish decisions.

Following *Vertical*, Ushev began work on his first official NFB film, *Tzaritza*; however, he became increasingly frustrated with the film and decided to take a break by making an entirely new film: *Tower Bawher*. Made in just three weeks, this was a landmark film for Ushev. His internet work had introduced him to the NFB, but *Tower* brought his name to festivals around the world, winning numerous prizes and acclaim.

Influenced by Russian constructivist artists like Dziga Vertov and the Stenberg brothers, and featuring the dynamic score *Time, Forward!* by Russian composer Georgy Sviridov — Canadian filmmaker Guy Maddin also used this score effectively in his short film *The Heart of the World* — a litany of lines, shapes, colors and sounds storm across and around the screen of *Tower Bawher*. They go up, they go down; they come together and just as quickly fall apart. *Tower Bawher* is an intense existentialist film about our often frustrating and restless drive to fight through the muddle and clutter of mediocrity and suppression in search of *the stuff* that makes *us*. In the end though, there is a paradox. No matter how far we climb or how much we seek, everything falls apart. Things come together, but only for a moment: that's the route of the ride.

For the record, "Bawher" is a bit of a nonsense word. "Tower in Russian is Baschnia," Ushev explains. "But because of the Cyrillic alphabet, a foreigner will read it like BAWHR, so Tower Bawher was perfect (Bauhaus, Bauer . . .)." Incredibly, *Tower Bawher* was made in just a few weeks. "I start doing it one night in April [2005]. I was in a deep depression. *Tzaritza* was not going well." During a particularly restless night, Ushev woke up and remembered an idea he had to use Sviridov's *Time, Forward!* "For many years," remembers Ushev, "this piece was the music for the evening news of the Soviet state TV. This program was broadcast every Friday."

While the television hummed in the background, Ushev's father would work on his own personal drawings and paintings, and also on more conventional propaganda posters that he made solely to earn a living. The memories of these Friday nights struck a chord with Ushev. "It was like an absurdist stage decoration. Before the news, there was usually a Russian children's programme on. Typically it featured very, very slow Russian animations like Norstein's *Hedgehog in the Fog*. I'd fall asleep immediately. Then, suddenly, I'd be awakened by the uplifting Sviridov music, with turning globes, and the lines of the dynamic building of Communism."

And so it was during a sleepless night in April that Ushev decided to make the movie. Five weeks later the finished film found its way to my desk. "I was not able to sleep during the entire process. It was like being in a trance, like I traveled back 30 years with a time machine. I didn't think about festivals, or if the movie will be finished. I was just diving into my memories, like a 'Cartesian theater'. It was like a letter. I was in a hurry to show it to my father, because I planned to make a short vacation in Bulgaria. It was done for him."

Before Ushev hit the road back to Bulgaria, he showed the film to producer Marc Bertrand. Bertrand liked the film immediately. "Théodore showed me the film with the Sviridov music," recalls Bertrand, "and I was really moved by the perfect 'marriage' between the picture and the music." When Bertrand asked Ushev what he planned on doing with *Tower*, Ushev had no answer. "My only goal was to show it to my father." Bertrand convinced him to finish the film with the NFB. "It felt natural," adds Bertrand, "to finish the film in the best condition possible and to finally produce it." Ushev agreed.

Bertrand showed the film around the NFB and everyone was impressed. There was just one problem: no one could determine who owned the copyright to the music. Sviridov had died in 1998 and according to a Copyright Board of Canada document dated September 13, 2005: "the person who inherited his copyright has since passed away . . . (and) that the copyright entitlement over the works of Sviridov is the object of a dispute before the Russian civil courts that will not be resolved for some time yet." After the Copyright Board of Canada rejected the application, the NFB decided to negotiate directly with the Russians.

"It became a nightmare," says Ushev, "but the NFB helped me enormously. Their entire legal department was involved into the process. It is really incredible how difficult is to deal with the Russians. Everything that seems easy becomes complicated. So, even when the bureaucrats tease an artist, he cannot live without them. It is like a family, they hate each other, but cannot live without. And the next morning are in love again."

Fortunately, the copyright issues — which somehow seem appropriate for a film that, in part, deals with the uneasy relationship between art and state — were solved just in time for *Tower* to have its world premiere in September 2005 at the Ottawa International Animation Festival.

Ushev credits the NFB for more than just taking on *Tower*: "Before starting at the NFB, animation was a hobby for me. I made internet movies, put them online and forgot about them. Suddenly I felt responsible. I couldn't do this movie if I was not working at NFB."

"*Tower Bawher* was a therapy," admits Ushev. "I did it to cure myself from my memories. Every child of an artist tries to escape from his mighty shadow, and to create his own world. And almost no child can do it."

Tower is more than just a search for self and an ode to a father: it is also a tribute to those artists who continually struggle to escape from the ominous and numbing shadows of bureaucracy and censorship. It's appropriate that *Tower* has become an NFB film. For over 60 years, the NFB has struggled, successfully and unsuccessfully, with that precarious relationship between artist and bureaucrat, and really, it's the struggle that counts. It's the struggle that is life.

In 2006, Ushev somehow found time to make three films. What's even more impressive is how different the films are in terms of technique and tone.

Tzaritza (meaning "seashell") was made for the NFB's *Talespinners* series. The object of the series was to present films that dealt with multicultural experiences from a child's perspective. Ushev chose to tell a story about a Canadian-born Bulgarian girl whose family visits Bulgaria to see her grandmother and learn more about her parents' native country. After they return home to Canada, the girl wishes that the Black Sea would move closer to their home so that her grandmother could join them.

Minus the annoying, shrill voice of the girl narrating, the film is one of Ushev's most accomplished (and upbeat) films — a luscious collage of luminous imagery that captures the wonder of being a child, when seemingly simple experiences captivate and thrill you. *Tzaritza* is a celebration of family, but it also touches on the difficulties in bringing two worlds together.

Ushev drew the inspiration from a Bulgarian family he knew in Montreal. "They were like a mirror to my family. My daughter was just born. It was a story about the usual and very common dysfunction in all immigrant families, where the child is born Canadian, and they are new arrivals."

Originally, Ushev wanted to explore the different perspectives of Bulgaria. "The child never completely understands the point of view of her father's and mother's, for her the other country is just a touristy, funny destination, but another place. For the parents, it is a place, full with emotions, and history. The only meeting point is the lovely grandmother."

The parents' perspective is largely absent from the film and Ushev was not at all pleased with this. "This was my first official NFB film and I didn't know how to deal with all the obstacles of bureaucracy. I don't like the final result. I wrote the story. But the producers insisted that professional scriptwriter come in. So he started putting in those stupid ice-cream stories, etc. Basically I've put more energy to fight for my ideas, than to make the film. At the end I was totally exhausted. I ended with almost all my original ideas, but all my energy was gone."

Sadly, the real girl's grandmother died one week before she was scheduled to visit her family in Montreal. "It was supposed to be her first arrival here," says Ushev, "and it was going to be put at the end of the film." After her death, Ushev told his friend that he wasn't going to finish the film but his friend disagreed. "He told me finish it," says Ushev, "because this will be the best thing for the memory of my mother. So this is why I put this end. The mother will never come to Montreal, and will never spend the Christmas with them, but she will be with them forever."

In 2006, NFB producer Michael Fukushima approached Ushev to tell him that Sony, Rogers (a Canadian cable company) and Bravo! (a Canadian TV channel) wanted some mobile film content. Ushev proposed "an idea about the bipolar nature of the seduction; how you hate someone and someplace, and still it seduces you and you miss it after."

It was a juxtaposition between a man, and a woman, cultures, noise and the calmness of Zen, dark and bright . . ." Fukushima approved the idea and less than three weeks later, Ushev handed him the film, *Sou* (which means "manic depressive" in Japanese and "unbearable noise" in Chinese).

Sou is based on Ushev's experience as a tourist in Japan. Using a collage of kitsch Japanese imagery, Ushev creates a feverish and maddening visual assault that perfectly conveys the exhausting, ignorant and whirlwind experience of a stranger in a strange land.

And for the grand finale of 2006, Ushev finally completed the film that had been following him since his web design days. During his time working for "all those shitty companies," Ushev decided that it was time to get a grip on his life, to stop wasting time being miserable and to get to the process of living. He found similar sentiments expressed in the writings of Franz Kafka, and in particular a story from *The Trial* about a man who waits behind a closed door guarded by a gatekeeper. "Kafka first wrote it as a short story," says Ushev, "and published it in a small local newspaper. I later discovered that the story is actually a very old Jewish tale that he just adapted. So, he is not even the author of it."

Behind the scenes, Susan Fuda, Ushev's producer from Valkyrie Films (the original producers of the film), not only managed to get the excerpt from Walter Ruttmann's film that appears at the beginning, but also received permission to use the music of the famous Estonian composer Arvo Pärt. "She arranged it for very little money," says Ushev. "Everybody was telling me that it wasn't possible, he never gives his music for animated films anymore. He wanted to see the film. We sent it and he gave me the rights."

The NFB had refused the film when Ushev initially proposed it in 2003, but finally Ushev decided to complete the film using his own money and what he'd been given from Valkyrie and Quebec's provincial government funding body Société de développement des entreprises culturelles (SODEC). When he was finished, he showed *The Man Who Waited* to Marc Bertrand. "I didn't expect them to take it," says Ushev. "I think they took it because basically it costs nothing. But I'm very grateful, they came in as co-producers and distributed the film internationally."

Highlighted by Pärt's haunting score, and woodcut-style drawings with rich red and black colors, *The Man Who Waited* is a beautiful expressionistic work that shifts Kafka's story about law to a more personal story about the search for truth. A man waits by the open door of truth that is guarded by a gatekeeper; he is told that he's not ready to go in. The man waits and waits. Before he dies, he is told that this was his door and that he could have gone in anytime he wanted. Instead, he has just waited for his entire life to find the truth and now it's too late.

"For me," says Ushev, "this my best film. I did everything that I wanted to in it. It contains all the feelings, and all the grief, and all the struggles of this time in my life, of eight months of happiness, fear, and despair."

Although *The Man Who Waited* didn't perform as well as *Tower Bawher*, it did win awards in Iran, Portugal, and Canada. Some critics have dismissed it as slow and boring; the striking contrast in pace and tones between the frantic rhythms of *Tower* and the contemplative mood of *The Man Who Waited* triggered some of the criticisms. *Tower* was a big festival success and people wanted more of that.

"It is slow," says Ushev, "because this is how the time was. Because it has all the feelings and fear that no matter how I think I control the life, it is always something or someone who rules my life and all the things that happen."

In 2007, Ushev was asked by the NFB to make a 3-D version of *Tower Bahwer*, but finding the process tedious, he started work on another film, *Drux Flux* (2008). Ushev's starting point was a book by German philosopher Herbert Marcuse called *One-Dimensional Man* (1964). Marcuse believed that consumerism is a form of social control and that we live in an authoritarian society where our perception of freedom is dictated by a few individuals. Marcuse believed that this industry would die, but that the people would all be the victims of the collapse.

Drux Flux is a tense and unrelenting work that smashes the viewer with the force of a hammer. Images of factories fill the screen and the tension builds and builds as more and more factories appear. Finally, the structures clash, collide and collapse, taking humanity with them.

Reminiscent of *Tower Bawher* (the use of Soviet constructivist imagery and a powerful score by Russian composer Alexander Mosolov) in parts, *Drux Flux* is a decidedly more cynical, almost nihilistic work that seems to offer little hope for society. Ushev, though, says that he believes there is hope in the end. "The good news is that everything collapses. This is how new things are built. Of course, it could turn out to be worse, but everything that is new at the beginning is inspiring."

Ushev's latest film *Lipsett Diaries* (2009), inspired by the life of the legendary Canadian experimental filmmaker, Arthur Lipsett (I should put it on record that I'm the scriptwriter for this film). During the winter of 2005, I forwarded Ushev an e-mail I had received from someone discussing the morals of artists. She mentioned Lipsett's name but, at that stage, Ushev had never heard of him. "I did a little research," explains Ushev, "and I found that he was very influential NFB director in the sixties. And absolutely by chance he lived on the same street in Montreal as me. I went there and met the concierge. He brought me to a big locker, where they were gathering all the unnecessary leftovers from the former tenants. I found a small notebook, blue, handwritten 'Lipsett' on it. I found everything inside this small notebook. Everything and nothing. Trying to reconstruct someone's life through those notes seemed impossible. This is how I decided to do this film."

For an artist who has become as respected and successful as Ushev has, he remains unsatisfied with his films — not that he thinks this is a bad thing. "I feel very good when I make a film, and enjoy this moment. They help me to know better myself and to see the things that I don't like in myself. But, once a film is finished, I don't care anymore about it. Up till now, I haven't made any film that I'm satisfied with. If I'm satisfied, it means that I'll have to stop making films."

Few animators have matched the passion and urgency of Théodore Ushev. His are not perfect films, but that's okay: art, like life, is flawed — that's the nature of existence. Ushev's films are always honest. That's what counts. He pushes himself and his viewers to look at and understand the flaws of their life and their society. His films are a refreshing and sorely needed dose of reality in a field dominated by works of faux angst and hollow technological "candy". Ushev doesn't make films to please you or me or Disney: he makes films because he has to.

For the sake of animation, let's hope that satisfaction and Théodore Ushev never meet.

Figure 11.1   Bob Sabiston

Figure 11.2   Drink Creatures

Figure 11.3   *Roadhead*

CHAPTER 11

Bob Sabiston

The Unanimator

Bob Sabiston is the only animator I know who apparently isn't an animator. The animation purists will tell you that his brand of digital rotoscoping (using his own Rotoshop software in, for example, *Waking Life* and *A Scanner Darkly*), amounts to little more than tracing over live-action images. These are the same people who consider Max and Dave Fleischer (Betty Boop and Popeye creators) as pioneers of animation even though they routinely used rotoscope animation in their films. What about Norman McLaren and his famous film *Neighbours*? Hell, didn't Ralph Bakshi make rotoscope films like *American Pop* in the 1980s? It was shot in live-action and sped up — is that really animation? Heck, is computer animation really animation?

Sabiston has heard the critics and . . . he agrees with them.

Wait a second . . . what's that?

"I agree with them," says Sabiston. "It's not really pure animation. But I've done pure animation, and it just never excited me very much. I like being able to take someone's real expression and magnify it, twist it, and amplify it. I realize that it's kind of a cheat, but to me, that just means you've got to use it to go further, to do more than you could even think of doing in regular animation. And I don't really care what it's called as long as it's something that looks cool or new."

Magnify, twist, and amplify: those are the key words and they are what make Sabiston's work as much a part of animation has McLaren and the Fleischers. Sabiston doesn't just trace over an image, he re-creates it, giving the image an entirely new life and meaning. Just take a look at his short film *Grasshopper* (2005). The film consists only of an interview with a man sitting on a park bench in New York. Sabiston recorded the interview with a digital camera and then dumped it on to a computer and used his software programme to animate it. "My girlfriend Holly and I were in New York interviewing people for a PBS [Public Broadcasting Service] project we did (*Topic Pot Pie*). A. J. Vadehra was one of the random people we approached, and I was so struck by his interview that I eventually decided to animate the whole thing."

The 14-minute film has no edits, but throughout this fascinating interview, there are subtle caricature-tinged changes being made to the man's face, along with alterations to Sabiston's unstable backgrounds. The changes often reflect the tone or topic that the man is discussing. If you take away Sabiston's software, you'd still be left with a relatively interesting person, but visually, the film would be about as captivating as a sigh.

Sabiston grew up a cartoon fan, but didn't start thinking about making them until he got into college. "I loved going to see these traveling film festivals like *Animation Celebration* and *Spike and Mike's Sick and Twisted Animation*, and I was really struck by Pixar's *Luxo Jr.* when it came out. The combination of humanistic emotion with the CG technology really wowed me."

In high school Sabiston had developed an interest in computer graphics and decided to study it at the Massachusetts Institute of Technology (MIT). "I got an undergraduate research job at the just-opened Media Lab, and at first I was just working on paint programs and still graphics. However by the third year I was writing animation software."

During that third year, Sabiston also made his first film, *Beat Dedication* (1988), about a battle between a robot drummer and a robot fly. "My little brother was into drumming," says Sabiston, "and I wanted to make an animation for him about a robot drummer." *Beat Dedication* was well received, selected for the Siggraph Computer Animation Festival and the World Animation Celebration in Los Angeles.

Sabiston's second film, *Grinning Evil Death* (1990), with fellow student Mike McKenna did even better. The film, which mixed drawn and computer animation, was accepted at Siggraph and, more importantly, it was selected for a new show by MTV called *Liquid Television*; the show brought Sabiston a lot of exposure and it was only then that he really felt he could make a career as an animator.

God's Little Monkey (1994) was even more successful, winning a prestigious Prix Ars Electronica Golden Nica award in 1994.

All three films are competent above-average works, but they haven't dated well because of advancements in computer technology. Frankly, if Sabiston's career had ended here, we'd be talking about someone else.

In a sense, Sabiston's career did end here; having moved to Austin, Texas, Sabiston was burned-out after working for two years on *God's Little Monkey*. "The process for this film was exhausting and I didn't know anyone else who could do it with me, so I got very discouraged with continuing to make animation.

I took a couple of years off, during which time I got into documentary films. When I decided to get back into animation in 1996, I knew I wanted to go interview some people and do some animated representation of that. I thought I would just do quick life-drawings of each frame and see what happened. I had to write a program to do it, though, just because I couldn't find one for sale."

As he starting making the first animation for his new project, *Project Incognito* (1997), Sabiston realized that, "I was basically drawing the same lines over and over for various facial features. It would save time to stitch those together across frames, allowing me to skip the frames that didn't change much from the frame before." With the birth of the interpolated rotoscope technique, Sabiston found his passion for animation and soon emerged as an innovative new voice in both animation and documentary.

Sabiston entered an MTV contest with *Project Incognito* and was awarded second place; MTV invited Sabiston to come to New York to make more 30-second interviews for *Project Incognito*.

Eager to use the technique for his own indie film, Sabiston left New York and returned to Austin. On the road trip home, Sabiston and a friend stopped in an assortment of towns and interviewed people; these interviews became the basis for his film *Roadhead*.

During the making of *Roadhead*, Sabiston also discovered a new way of working. Before *Project Incognito*, Sabiston admits that because he was very controlling about his films, he wasn't good at working with other people; however, when MTV hired another artist to work with him, Sabiston enjoyed the experience because of his new technique. "I found that the way we were using the rotoscoping technique, changing styles every few seconds, really made it easy to accommodate other artists. So back in Austin with *Roadhead* I put up flyers and got all these artists to come into my house and help me animate the film. That experience formed the template for almost all the work we've done since."

In *Roadhead* we are dropped into the middle of a conversation. Sabiston uses a mix of color sequences and black and white interviews. The animation adds a level of caricature and edge, making quiet comments on the characters as they talk. The face of a black guy being interviewed constantly changes styles from clean, smooth to unstable, sketch style. Eyes expand on other characters. The shapes of their heads alter, revealing — in an admittedly extreme manner — how people change forms when they express themselves. Their appearances change so rapidly that we're never really sure what these people really look like.

Technique aside, *Roadhead* is a fascinating document of the American experience as told by compelling yet fractured voices from society's fringes: a bank robber, an unemployed woman, a guy obsessed with *The Dukes of Hazzard*, a waitress and a few other borderline head cases.

The animation is clearly in its primitive stages with *Roadhead*, but it already anticipates many of the traits of Sabiston's later films: the caricatures, floating backgrounds and a genuine love of people who walk the border of articulate and wing nut.

Having worked primarily with black-and-white, Sabiston brought out the colors for his next film, *Snack and Drink* (1999). This 3-minute short stars a 13-year-old autistic kid named Ryan

Power; the film consists of Ryan's visit to a corner store to get a, you guessed it, snack and drink.

In *Snack and Drink* colors add another dimension to the image, turning it into a floating painting. Sabiston continues his fascination with people on the margins of society — a subject rarely explored in animation. "Well, I went through a phase in my late twenties where I really tried to break out of my shell and interact with other people, including strangers, as much as I could," says Sabiston. "That was about the time I started doing the rotoscoping. So some of those films are the result of me just approaching strangers with a camera and striking up conversation. I'm a big fan of Errol Morris too, and he always finds fascinating people for his documentaries. After all, if you're going to animate real people, they should probably be the most interesting people you can find, don't you think?"

Sabiston remained friends with Ryan and made a second film with him in 2008; *The Even More Fun Trip* follows Ryan and Sabiston during a day at a theme park. "We go out to eat the second Wednesday of each month," says Sabiston. "A few times we've gone to theme parks together. Animating one of these trips is something that we at Flat Black Films [Sabiston's film company] had discussed and even attempted before — theme parks seem to be his favorite places on earth, and the colorful rides and crowds of people seem like good subject material for animation."

During this particular visit, Ryan decides that he must repeat exactly what he did the first time they went to the theme park. He insists on taking the same rides in the same order, sitting down at the same table and eating the same meal. The film runs over 20 minutes and captures the fun, strangeness and frustration of spending the day with Ryan. By the end of the film, you feel as burned-out as Sabiston does. Ryan's a swell kid, but you can only take so much — and that might be the downside to the film. It's a tough work to sit through and it starts to get on your nerves after a while so, depending on your perspective, *The Even More Fun Trip* is an accurate and pained portrait of autism or a film that overstays its welcome. The theme park provides Sabiston with a dazzling set for his rotoscoping and captures the dizziness, frenzy, excitement, fear and fatigue of an emotional and busy public place.

One of Sabiston's friends, Tommy Pallotta, introduced the animator to filmmaker Richard Linklater (*Slacker* and *Dazed and Confused*). The two friends approached Linklater to work on an animated documentary TV show in the vein of *Roadhead*. The idea didn't pan out, but Linklater approached Sabiston later with the idea for a feature film, *Waking Life*. Linklater liked the look of Sabiston's animation and felt it would be a perfect match for his film; Linklater's observation was spot on. *Waking Life* turned out to be the perfect project for Sabiston's style.

Sabiston's animation in *Waking Life* serves a variety of technical and conceptual purposes for Linklater. First, the rotoscope technique complements the ambiguous dream/reality duality of the film: it's reality and yet it's not. Secondly, the animation serves as a visual springboard into the minds of the various characters, bringing their theories and perspectives to life. Finally, the animation becomes an active participant in the film in that it caricatures the characters as they speak. Different artists were used for each scene, giving each space and character a unique personality. This adds another layer of existential fragmentation while, at times, playfully poking fun at some of the characters. At the same time, the lack of a cohesive style along with the shifting, floating, dislocated backgrounds and landscapes keeps the viewer on edge, at a distance.

Sabiston found the experience of working on *Waking Life* exhilarating. "It was great. That was exactly the kind of animated movie I wanted to make — very adult, very unusual, and lots of faces to animate. It was a really organic, natural evolution from the shorts we'd been making."

Linklater shot and edited the original footage and oversaw the artists, but gave Sabiston an unusual amount of creative freedom. "I think he saw the whole thing as a big experiment," says Sabiston. "He just sort of loosely guided the thing, occasionally asking for something specific or for certain scenes to be done in a different way."

Waking Life was a critical success internationally, with the non-animated world heaping praise on Sabiston's technique. Even more impressive was the diversity of awards that the film received: aside from the Grand Prix for feature animation at the 2002 Ottawa International Animation Festival, *Waking Life* also received an experimental film award from the National Society of Film Critics and a "regular' feature award from the Venice Film Festival. Sabiston was even named Digital Effects Artist of the Year by the American Film Institute.

Waking Life was, somewhat surprisingly, largely overlooked in the animation world. The Academy ignored *Waking Life* when they voted for Best Animated Feature — beaten out by such epics as Disney's *Lilo & Stitch*. Inside and outside the Academy there were hermetic factions who, like the embarrassed parents of a troubled kid, refused to acknowledge this hybrid animation freak film as a part of their world.

Linklater invited Sabiston to work with him again, this time on a feature adaptation of Philip K. Dick's famous novel *A Scanner Darkly*. Unfortunately, Sabiston's stay was short and not particularly sweet.

"We left (me and the four lead animators)," says Sabiston, "because it was impossible to animate that movie in the style Rick wanted for less than $4 million in one year. They insisted that we kill ourselves to do it for $2 million in six months, and we said no. We walked out over the abusive treatment we'd been receiving during those first three months of animation. We'd been fighting with them the whole time about the time/money issue. I don't think they really believed or trusted that we were doing it the best and cheapest way possible already."

Adding further insult, the *Scanner* filmmakers continued to use Sabiston's software. "I never would have allowed *Scanner* to use my software without me, but the Warner Brothers' legal team threatened me with multi-million dollar lawsuits if I obstructed their movie, and everyone I consulted said I would lose if I tried to fight them."

The time spent on *Scanner* wasn't an entire waste for Sabiston: he spent six months making many improvements to his software. "We really wanted to reduce the 'wobbliness' that many people disliked about *Waking Life*, and we had that whole scramble suit to conquer [the scramble suit allows the story's narcotic agents to distort their appearance beyond recognition]. We went through so many iterations on that suit. I added things like masking, where one layer can mask another, letting you cut holes in objects.

I also added this warp-tool, letting you stretch one layer of animation into another four-sided quadrilateral. It made it easier to rotoscope changes in camera perspective."

Sabiston admits that the final film looks good, but says, "I'm glad I didn't have to go through that hell and I think the way we were treated was almost criminal." Sabiston was particularly annoyed that his animation colleagues Patrick Thornton, Randy Cole, Katy O'Connor and Jennifer Drummond received nothing but "an additional animation" credit, even though they were pivotal to the film's animation.

Shot in Sabiston's backyard, *Yard* (2001) lovingly captures the summer sounds of cicadas. This minimalist film allowed Sabiston to get back to just making his own work and to further develop his technique. In one scene, the leaves move to the rhythms of the wind and the song of the cicadas; unlike the effective but discombobulated seasickness feeling of Sabiston's previous films, these movements are smooth, calm and precise. "These shots," says Sabiston, "use another software technique I was developing, in which each little shape is guided across the screen in real-time, rather than the frame-by-frame drawing used in most animation. If you look at a single shape it is kind of wonky and inexact, but in aggregate the motion of hundreds of these shapes captures the overall motion pretty well."

Sabiston then made another foray of sorts into feature films: this time, he contributed to Lars von Trier's experimental documentary, *The Five Obstructions* (2003). Trier loved the film *The Perfect Human* (1967), made by his friend Jørgen Leth. Trier challenged Leth to remake the film five times, but with a condition: each time there must be an obstruction given by Trier. Trier's fourth obstruction was to have Leth remake *The Perfect Human* in animation. "I got a call out of the blue from Jørgen Leth's son, wanting to know if we could do 5 minutes of animation in a month," says Sabiston. "They sent us the edited video that they wanted animated, along with a bunch of extra footage to use as background material."

Leth was not a big fan of cartoons, so Sabiston instead gave the film the look of a comic book, using lush colors and story panels. Leth and his son visited Sabiston to review their style sheets and were delighted with the work. "I was really proud when I saw our animation in the film," says Sabiston. "They really used us as kind of a plot-device, defeating the evil Von Trier just when he thought he had won the wager! That project was really a joy."

Currently, Sabiston is working on a few different projects: *Fuzzy Town* is a 5-minute trailer for a feature or TV series written by Sabiston's friends David and Nathan Zellner. *Line Research* is an ongoing pet project that uses animation performed live. He also recently completed a series of web animations for comic-artist David Rees's *Get Your War On* and is at work on a paint and animation program for the Nintendo DS gaming system. "It is the sort of thing I would have wanted as a kid. It lets you make little drawings and animations and publish them wirelessly to the web."

Sabiston has frequently been approached by animators interested in buying his software and admits he's surprised that no one has ripped it off yet. "I don't really want to sell it myself though — not only because it would be a pain in the ass, but also because the look would be everywhere. Who knows, though. If someone else rips it off, then I'll probably make some effort to compete — if I can do it without it consuming all my time."

It's a shame really that Sabiston has not been given more credit in the animation world as an innovator and pioneer for pushing the medium into new territories. "I know that sometimes you can capture something on camera that is very real, or rare — a moment of sincerity or humor, and those are the things most worth spending the time to animate," says Sabiston. "I think it works similarly when you see something in a performance that others might not see due to some distracting element in the video. You can use the rotoscoping to draw attention to the qualities you see there."

Sabiston's hybrid animation creates a unique collision between reality and fantasy, revealing an anxious, absurd and unreal world that also has the very real and wacky sensation of living.

Figure 12.1   Bruce Alcock

Figure 12.2   *Quinte Hotel*

Figure 12.3   *Vive la Rose*

CHAPTER 12

Bruce Alcock
The Storyteller

Canadian animator Bruce Alcock has only made three independent films, but what a trio of work he has created. Using a mixture of high and low techniques including a distinct use of found objects, Alcock's work is a celebration of voices and stories of the past and present. Whether it's a crazy phone machine message, a poetry reading or a sad song of lost love, Alcock's work reminds us of the importance of keeping stories, voices and traditions alive — without them, our lives drift into nothingness.

Alcock was born in Corner Brook, Newfoundland, a small paper mill town of about 24,000 people. Alcock's animation roots date back to grade five when his friend Nick's mother came to his class to teach art. "One of her lessons," remembers Alcock, "involved bleaching film, then drawing on it with permanent markers and projecting the result." Inspired by the film and their mutual love of drawing, the two friends started a small film club with a few other friends. "[We] made tons of animated stuff," says Alcock, "pixilation, clay, cut-out (including a grade 11 physics film), mostly about fighting and destruction by fire."

Alcock also spent considerable time at the local office of the National Film Board of Canada, watching many of the studio's acclaimed animation films. "We were starved for material, and

watched pretty much the whole library of animation," notes
Alcock. "McLaren was the big favourite, but other highlights
included *Sand Castle* [by Co Hoedeman], *Spinnolio* [by John
Weldon], *The Sweater* [by Sheldon Cohen], and Kaj Pindal's
stuff. It blows me away that we could watch all that material on
film, for free."

After high school, Alcock studied tuba at the University of
Toronto. He then moved to Paris to learn French, did a compara-
tive literature degree at the University of Toronto, then moved
to Barcelona and taught English. In Barcelona, Alcock met an
animator named Dirk Van de Vondel. "We both went to a life
drawing club. He needed help on a spot, then a short, and then a
couple more spots. I ended up apprenticing with him: started out
artworking, then in-betweening, then animating. The work was
very physical — charcoal, pastel, paint — and the drawings were
extremely loose and textural. Really inspiring, fine art looking
work. Perhaps the best learning aid was the fact that he had no
shooting or previewing equipment at all. For months, I watched
all movement a few frames at a time by flipping paper, trying to
imagine how it would all work on film. He'd send the stuff away
to be shot as we finished each job, but I saw nothing until about
nine months after we'd started working together. At that point, all
my previsualizations coalesced at once. Very exciting moment."

Alcock returned to Toronto in 1990 and briefly attended
Sheridan College. "I hated it. Animation history seemed to be
limited to American commercial studio work." After his short stay
at Sheridan, Alcock, along with partner Adam Shaheen, formed
the now acclaimed animation studio Cuppa Coffee in 1991.

In 1995 Alcock moved to Chicago to take charge of Tricky

Pictures, a studio that emerged out of an old deal between Cuppa Coffee and US studio Backyard Productions. "[Backyard] offered for us [Cuppa Coffee] to go into business with them," Alcock told Canada's *Playback Magazine* in 2000, "and I decided to take them up on it and go down [to Chicago]. Adam [Shaheen] continued with Cuppa Coffee."

Five years later, Alcock and his then wife, animator/filmmaker Anne Marie Fleming, decided to leave the windy chill of Chicago and return to Canada. This time they settled in Vancouver and started the studio Global Mechanic, which Alcock continues to run today.

Alcock's first contact with the great Canadian poet Al Purdy came in 1983 while the poet was a writer-in-residence at the University of Toronto. "I went with my roommate Alex Pugsley to hear Purdy do a reading. [It was] such a pleasure to hear irreverent, casual rants and meanderings in that bizarre voice. Alex and I imitated Purdy's voice a lot afterwards. Nine years later when I returned from Barcelona I applied for a Canada Council grant to make the film. At the time I was thinking of Yeats or Hopkins, but Alex suggested Purdy and *At the Quinte Hotel*.

Alcock chose *At the Quinte Hotel* "because it's a poem about poetry in an unusual context, because it's visceral and casual, because it's patently Canadian. And I love mixing animation and poetry in general because both media are to a large extent solitary at the time of production, they're both obsessively worked out, detailed, exacting, yet at the same time expressive, loose, gestural and rhythmic. This poem was particularly well suited to the way I wanted to animate because it's about the collision of beauty and ugliness, art and everyday life. I worked throughout at balancing beauty in the image with rawness, not over-aestheticizing the poem, and keeping the technique and look gestural, off-the-cuff like the language of the poem."

Initially, Alcock planned on getting Purdy (who died in 2000 at age 81) to do a reading of the poem. "We went to visit him and his wife Eurithe in Ameliasburg, Ontario, but he was far too ornery, and left us in a huff, saying 'my wife'll make you chili an' toast.' We had brought a bottle of whiskey for him. After chili, toast, and a few illuminating (if a bit depressing) stories about her life with Al, Eurithe said goodbye and 'thanks for the liquor, boys.'"

Instead, Alcock settled on a reading of the poem that Purdy gave at the first Congress of Canadian Poets in Toronto in 1968. "Michael Ondaatje was there, Earle Birney, Irving Layton — all the big guys," says Alcock. "So it's a reading among peers. It's a poor reading from a pure performance perspective: his rhythm and diction are all over the place, his timing is weird. But you can hear Al Purdy saying his poem out loud to his friends and enemies: it's a poet reading his own stuff, not a performer recording a reading for a film."

Given the circumstances of Alcock's initial visit to Purdy's home, getting the rights for the poem was surprisingly easy. "[Purdy] was pretty clearly dubious about the likelihood of the idea going anywhere, grudgingly flattered that I wanted to do it at all, and happy to agree to it for 10 percent of any revenue to come from the film. Very sadly, he died before I made the film. I had lost his approval letter in the mean time, so I called his widow Eurithe to ask again. She put me on to his executor and publisher, who was a little prickly about the whole affair. It took a while, but we got permission for a fee. The reading is the property of the

CBC Archives, so we negotiated a price for ten years of rights."

Funding for *At the Quinte Hotel* (2005) was derived primarily from the Global Mechanic coffers. "I got a $6,000 grant from the Canada Council in 1992, which I spent on rent for the first two months of Cuppa Coffee when Adam and I started out, on supplies, mag transfer of the DAT recording, and prep work. Then I was too busy to do the film: it stayed on the shelf, flames of guilt licking over the mouldering stack of animation paper. Then I made *Wrong Number Phone Message* (2004) to jump-start myself, using commercial revenue. We basically paid the animators for five weeks on the job, but had them work one of those weeks on the film. It worked about the same on *Quinte* — a certain percentage of job revenue went to the film instead of into profit."

While getting *Quinte* prepared, Alcock returned home one night to find a rather strange message on his answering machine. "I got a very odd wrong number phone message," says Alcock, "the phone message demanded I do something with it. It seemed like a small enough project to jump-start me into the next one, or that's how I justified it at the time, so I made *Wrong Number Phone Message* using the message as the sound track." In the message, a crazy old man living in the woods of the Pacific Northwest calls a woman named Sarah (whom Alcock doesn't know) and gives her hell for siccing the "city" on him to clean up his property. Using an array of materials including berries, wood, dolls, leaves and assorted junk, Alcock visualizes the life of this man unhinged.

Meanwhile, Purdy's widow was sent a copy of *At the Quinte Hotel*, but Alcock still isn't sure if she's seen it yet. "I'd love to know," says Alcock, "but she preferred not to be contacted. It must be pretty tough to survive a relatively famous spouse, then have to deal with them calling and asking for things."

At the Quinte Hotel is a dizzying mixed-media gem that uses sundry techniques to explore the repressive and contradictory shortcomings of masculinity, along with the clash between so-called high (flowers, beauty) and low (bars, beer, fistfights) culture. A poet sits in a bar "drinking beer with yellow flowers in underground sunlight." The bartender ignores the poet's mumblings and a fight breaks out, blocking the poet's way to the toilet; he jumps one of the men and beats the shit out of him. While he sits on the pummeled little guy he asks him "Would you believe I write poems?" The poet then reads one of his poems to the crowd in the bar. When he finishes the poem, people in the crowd cry and everyone shakes his hand. "It was a heartwarming moment for literature," says the poet. However, when the poet tries to get a free beer for his poetry reading, he's refused. He realizes sadly that "it was brought home to me in the tavern that poems will not really buy beer or flowers or a goddamn thing."

With *Quinte* in the can, Alcock turned to something quite different: he contributed 40 minutes of animation to a theater/ poetry/dance/animation show called *The Four Horsemen Project*. "The animation," says Alcock, "was mixed typography and drawings, projected onto the back wall and floor while dancers moved, sang and spoke to the work of the Four Horsemen, concrete poets of the late sixties. Some of the animation played on its own, some was tangentially related to the performers, other bits interacted directly."

Back in the studio, Alcock continued (and continues) to direct and supervise various TV commercials, TV series and art projects.

"Lately we're working on *FETCH! with Ruff Ruffman* for PBS, developing a couple of shows, commercials for American Express and B&W speakers, a PSA in support of Darfur and the print design work for *Vive la Rose*."

This last project, *Vive la Rose* (2009), is Alcock's most recent film. On the seashores of Newfoundland, the camera takes the viewer into a shack and inside, a drawer opens to reveal three compartments. A man begins singing a song of lost love; his voice is old and fragile — he has lived and suffered. In the main compartment, the tragic love story is told in drawn animation. In the second compartment "real" objects from the story appear. Then handwritten lyrics appear on the screen. When the song ends, dirt covers the drawer. We leave and return to the seashore. Life goes on.

Vive la Rose is a beautiful, haunting ode to lost love, mortality and the brutal conditions that Newfoundland fishermen often endure. The film is also a reminder of the power and importance of indigenous stories. The sea and land — impenetrable, majestic, murderous and uncaring — goes on; without our stories, we do not.

Alcock first heard *Vive la Rose* on an old cassette tape while he was driving. "I had to pull over because I found it so sad. From early on, I pictured this solitary old fisherman who had lived his life in regret over unrequited love. The singer is Émile Benoit, a French Newfoundland fiddler/singer/composer known almost as well for his libido as his music. He was 92 when he recorded the song; his fractured voice and unusual French add a lot of emotional depth to the song. The recording was a perfect conduit for my homesickness and representation of place."

Alcock's use of mixed-media and specifically object animation in the film is highlighted by his apparent love of real or found objects. He attributes this love of objects to his Newfoundland roots. "There's a certain pride in resourcefulness in Corner Brook, in using what's available to make your environment. I've always been drawn to the practical in art — Paterson Ewen's router landscapes come to mind — combining drawn representation with physical elements. Things that inform and take you outside of the content. I like the idea of simultaneous multiple perspectives, in representation as much as in conversation, the way they collide and buoy one another up."

Although Alcock has only just finished *Vive la Rose*, he's already at work on a new film. "It's a sort of Robert Breer vamp on a story my Great Aunt Vera used to tell. It's about a dogsled ride she took in 1919 in Newfoundland. I shot 16 mm black-and-white live-action footage of her telling the story in 1986, which I'll place in various parts of a black frame, then fill the negative space with animation. There's some stop-motion using domestic objects from the time as placeholders for story elements (she's a wooden clothes peg, the sled is a netmaker's shuttle), some line drawings, rotoscoping over footage from a snowmobile trip that matches the one in her story, photo collage and drawn snippets of my memories of time we spent together."

Global Mechanic's tagline is "making art work". So far, Alcock has done just that, striking an almost perfect balance between creating innovative commercial projects and personal work. "I originally went into commercial animation to fund my own film projects. Even though it took a while to get it to happen, it's working now and definitely will continue to."

Figure 13.1   *Switchcraft*

Figure 13.2   *The Round-About*

Figure 13.3   *Die Hard*

CHAPTER 13

The Tricks, Flies and Timing of Konstantin Bronzit

Konstantin Bronzit was born in Leningrad — later renamed St. Petersburg — in 1965. Bronzit's parents were modest people: his mother worked as a nurse, and his father worked as an optics mechanic creating optical devices for the military. The family's apartment overlooked a nearby church. The view inspired young Konstantin: "From the window of our apartment you could see the magnificent view of the beautiful Nicholskaya Church and its bell tower," recalls Bronzit. "I repeatedly drew educational sketches of the view from my apartment window."

Bronzit's interest in animation began early: "When I was in second grade my friend had showed me 'a trick' with his notebook. On each page was drawn a figure. Then — like a flipbook — the pages were quickly thumbed through, and the figures came to life." Bronzit was mesmerized by the trick and decided to try it himself. "Like a madman, I filled notebooks with dozens of drawings, contriving and animating my stories."

His fourth-grade art teacher recognized the young Russian's drawing talents, and suggested he be enrolled in a specialized art school. His parents agreed and from grades 5 to 11, he studied at a variety of art schools within St. Petersburg's Academy of Arts.

During these years, Bronzit's enthusiasm for animation remained. "I visited the movie theater located across the street from school. There I saw the Walt Disney collection and got inspired again! I would skip class and I was bewitched as I looked at the screen and listened to the laugh of the audience in the auditorium. Then I understood that *I wished to do the same thing*!"

Two years after graduating in 1983, Bronzit found work at Lennauchfilm. "They produced educational and popular science films about the hazards of smoking and used animation to explain the principles of gas movement, or made animated military maps."

As with all Soviet institutions, Lennauchfilm's work was strictly scheduled and they were expected to produce a certain number of films each year. While the studio provided Bronzit with practical animation experience, it was hardly a place for him to explore his creative ambitions. "The studio had its own in-house directors who had been working there for many years. The position of director was a long-service bonus achievement. They had no plans to give this 'warm' place to somebody young," says Bronzit. "I think that when I reached my forties maybe they would have entrusted me to make a short film representing the danger of nicotine to horses or something like that."

In 1988 Bronzit did get a chance to direct his first film; *The Round-About* is a better-than-average first film about the cyclical nature of power. A frog chases a fly until a bird comes along and chases the frog. Finally, a hunter appears and chases the bird. In the end, the fly returns and pesters the hunter until he runs off.

During perestroika there were many independent studios established: one of the first was Pilot Animation Studios. "The heads of the studio, Alexander Tatarski and Anatoli Prokhorov, were looking for the young, creative talents and, having seen my independent works, suggested that I create a film for the Pilot Studios. I continued to work in St. Petersburg and once a month visited Moscow to show the footage. As a result, during a few years I made several films under the name of the Pilot Studios."

Fare Well (1993) and *Pacifier* (1994) were Bronzit's first films for Pilot. "At that time I was keen on a caricature in newspapers and magazines. It taught me to think quickly, contrive laughable situations, and make gags. These types of films are typical for the director who is just starting out — funny and without claim to be treated as 'the serious art'. Evidently, those caricatures influenced my first films."

In 1994, a studio named ZIS was formed in St. Petersburg and Bronzit was offered an opportunity to make his early comic masterpiece, *Switchcraft*. The film, which won the Grand Prix at the 1995 Annecy International Animation Festival, recounts a rather bizarre evening experienced by a man and his cat as they try to sleep. "*Switchcraft* came up from a caricature," says Bronzit. "The person had put a mousetrap in front of a hole in the wall of his room. There is a shot glass of vodka as bait for the mousetrap. The walls of this room are decorated with trophies in the form of human hands precisely holding the same shot glasses. Although the plot of the film is about something totally different, an empty room with a lonely person and a mousetrap led me to the film."

In 1997, Bronzit was on the move again: a new studio named Melnitsa was formed in a sound recording studio that was operated by Bronzit's first employer, Lennauchfilm. "In order to declare itself a new talented studio," says Bronzit, "Melnitsa producers decided to make a series for TV. The series had to consist of very short and easy-to-execute films. I devised a plot of film parodies of well-known American blockbusters." The result was a 1-minute parody of the Bruce Willis film *Die Hard*. In just over a minute, Bronzit managed to summarize the entire vacuous plot of the Hollywood film.

Before Bronzit could get busy with Melnitsa, he headed to France after winning a competition to be an artist-in-residence at the acclaimed studio, Folimage. "By that time it was almost impossible to get funding for production. The storyboards of the film had been stored at the Pilot Studios for about a year. Suddenly, I received an invitation from the Folimage Studio to submit any of my work for the competition. I thought — why not? I sent *Ends of the Earth*, won the competition and went to France to make the movie."

In this impeccably timed comedy, an old Russian couple live with their cat, dog and cow in a small house that just happens to be located on the tip of a big mountain. "At the beginning there was a small house on the peak of the mountain," says Bronzit about the film's origins. "But the small house is not a script yet. I intuitively felt the comic opportunities concealed in this situation. The script was developed slowly, step by step. First there appeared a woman with the cow and a dog, and then the story fleshed out in my head."

By the time Bronzit returned to Russia in 1999, Melnitsa was beginning to work on commissioned TV projects. "I tried to help our young studio in every way," says Bronzit. "My work could, perhaps, be defined as the art director of the studio." Melnitsa developed quickly and, with state support and contracts from

Russian TV, became one of the first studios in Russia to produce feature animation films. While Bronzit has worked on a variety of commercial projects for the studio, he has found time to continue his independent career.

His most recent short, *The God* (2004), is a return, of sorts, to the pest of *The Round-About*. The multi-armed Hindu god Shiva is — as usual — just hanging around, until a fly begins to pester him. "From the beginning," says Bronzit, "I saw an image — a statue of the Indian deity irritated by the ordinary small housefly. In fact, everyone is familiar with this situation. From the beginning, I intended this film as a plastic etude with semantic zest."

The God was also Bronzit's first attempt at computer animation. "At first I thought that I would use puppet animation, but how could I execute the fly? Should it be on a string? I was looking for a complete representation of reality: the 'true' Bronze statue and the 'real' living fly. I figured that without modern technology I would not be able to manage this. I understood that the film should be three-dimensional, as the image of the Indian deity is always represented in the form of a statuette."

Although Bronzit denies that he has a familiar "style", the one constant throughout is his masterful comic timing. "For me this subject is special," says Bronzit. "I already had it within me long before I understood its precise meaning. Hardly understanding how to make a movie, I conceived *The Round-About*. The years passed, I made some more films and when I got to Pilot I heard this strange word 'timing'. Everyone repeated it over and over again 'timing, timing', but nobody could explain to me or tell me what this means in a movie. Now I wonder how have I made my movies? Probably, I just had inner flair."

Having just completed his most recent film, 2008 Academy Award nominee *Lavatory Lovestory* (about a lonely lavatory attendant who discovers flowers in her tip container), Bronzit has no plans for future projects and is relishing a good night's sleep again. He knows that this will soon change; that in a moment a flash will appear and it will begin again. We will be waiting.

Figure 14.1　Suzan Pitt

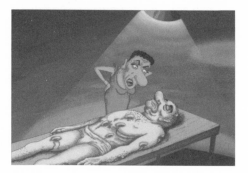

Figure 14.2　Woman cursing man

Figure 14.3　Doc and girl on horse

CHAPTER 14

Suzan Pitt

Dollhouses, Magic and Sexy Asparagus

Suzan Pitt didn't know it at the time, but her love of art and animation began in her childhood in her parent's house in Kansas, Missouri: "There was a dollhouse in the dark attic where I would go to play," says Pitt, "It was the thrill of setting the known world askew that was the most fun. I projected myself into plastic figures, chairs, lamps and various objects. It was an escape to a richer world of play and imagination."

A typical '50s teen, Pitt hung out with "flat top boyfriends," drank and smoked as she scoured around in search of drama and purpose. When she wasn't hanging out, she found solace in her room by drawing self-portraits and studying herself in the mirror. "I think I could affirm my person, by doing this — some were nude and some were pensive portraits staring into the mirror, transferred to paper. I never showed these to anyone, even though my mother was always rifling through my stuff to find artwork she could show her friends."

Pitt studied painting and printmaking at Cranbrook Academy of Art and graduated with a BFA in 1965; however, Pitt wasn't pleased with the school or her studies. It took Pitt years of intro-spection (and pot smoking) to find her confidence and voice again. "The lingo of art-speak can drain a person's ability to access the inner imagination. This conflict of making and speaking has followed me through the years — on the one hand the ability to verbalize and communicate about art is valuable, particularly in a teaching context, but on the other hand the artist's true desires, true self, has to rise privately."

Lost in thought, Pitt thought of her Kansas dollhouse and the vivid worlds and characters she had created in it as a child. How could she capture that world in her art? One day it occurred to her that her painted images looked like they were in arrested movement. "They had been somewhere and were about to go somewhere. I thought of doing animation, but didn't know anything about it. I had to make a pest of myself at various parties, suddenly switching the conversation to ask a filmmaker, 'Could you tell me how to put sound on my film?'"

While living in Minneapolis with her then husband Al Kraning, Pitt got a hold of an 8 mm Bolex camera. "With the Bolex mounted on a tripod taped to the floor, I animated cut-outs, paper paintings of living stuff (twigs and sprouts and unknown vegetables) moving through real grass I had made a bed for on the floor — that was it — an event."

When Pitt told her artist pals in Minneapolis that she was experimenting with animation, they frowned upon it: animation wasn't fine art in their oh-so-sophisticated minds. Pitt didn't care. She was convinced that she'd finally found the ideal vehicle to use as an artist, an art form that could capture the complexity of identity and imagination.

During the early 1970s, while teaching in Minneapolis, Pitt made a number of short animations: the first significant film is *Crocus* (1971), a cut-out film that anticipates many of the themes of Pitt's later works. A nude woman examines herself in the mirror (as Pitt used to do in her bedroom years before). Becoming aroused as she brushes her nipples, she closes the blinds and returns to the mirror; a naked man enters the room with a mighty erection. The couple begins to "get it on" until they're interrupted by a child's voice. After the mother gets up to comfort the child, she returns to the bed and as the couple make love, a parade of images (fruits, vegetables, moths, birds, a Christmas tree) float through the room.

Pitt articulates the difficulties of her life, specifically her failing marriage and life as a lover, wife, mother and artist. Pitt's use of cut-out animation creates a wooden, artificial atmosphere where marital sex has become awkward and jerky. The surreal imagery parade seems to represent the woman's repressed fervent imagination and desires: how can she juggle the complexities of being a lover, mother and artist?

Another early highlight is *Jefferson Circus Songs* (1973), a bizarre pixilation/cut-out film featuring kids and set in a circus. The painted backdrops and settings add a theatrical dimension to the film (a medium that Pitt would explore later in her career), while the pixilated imagery, piano accompaniment and unusual environment recall silent films and anticipate the work of Canadian filmmaker Guy Maddin.

Jefferson Circus Songs took Pitt a year to complete. "It was my first time working with actors and there was little time to work with ideas. There was a great deal of pressure working in a situation like that. You have to dig down no matter what, even if everything isn't perfect."

After Pitt's marriage collapsed, she and her son, Blue, moved to Amsterdam for a year in 1973. "Blue rode on the back of my bicycle to his new-age school and we both lived a kind of bohemian life there. Blue dressing in fantasy clothes and me making art and trying to earn a living by teaching animation at the art school in Den Haag. There was a lot of drugs and Amsterdam was a lively place with folks camped out in the Vondelpark getting stoned and the regular Dutch people just walking past on their way to work."

During that time, Pitt started on a storyboard for what would eventually be her next film, *Asparagus* (1979). "I had a small show at the Stedelijk Museum of artwork for my films and had an offer from an art printing place to produce a print — instead I asked to do a book of ink drawings for *Asparagus*. It turned into a kind of graphic novel — and during the course of making the book I worked out a design and construction for a film."

After completing the book, Pitt sent it to the American Film Institute and received her first grant. She also returned to the US to accept a teaching job at Harvard.

Asparagus (1979) marks Pitt's arrival on the animation and film circuit; this bold, luscious and overwhelming work is a giant step from her earlier films. Taking some of the visual aspects of *Crocus*, *Asparagus* is a journey through the creative process of a female artist. Like *Crocus*, the film begins with a woman in front of a mirror, only this time she's about to sit on the toilet and crap out some asparagus! Asparagus grows in her lavish garden (at one point a hand reaches down and sensually strokes an asparagus spear) alongside a lavish display of fruits and vegetables. Back inside the house there is a dollhouse with no borders from the real world. Images dominate this woman's existence, mingling with and altering the universe she inhabits. There is no distinction between the real and imagined: everything is there for the taking.

The woman eventually dons a mask, packs her bag full of images and goes out to give a performance in front of an audience.

After the performance, the woman returns home and removes her mask. Now faceless, she performs fellatio on an asparagus spear. It's less a sexual act then an exchange of ideas and imagery: The woman's mouth gives and receives. It's as though she is being recharged, having given herself up during her performance.

The pacing of the film is deliberately slow, giving the viewer a dream-like sensation. And like a dream, you can enter the film at any point and the meaning remains unchanged. "The film is a circle more than a straight-ahead experience," adds Pitt. "The taking in and spewing out, the searching and the discovering, the desire and the contact, the ever-evolving acts of nature."

Like a work of free jazz, Pitt's imagery is open to multiple interpretations. The downside of the film's freewheeling nature is that, over the years, *Asparagus* has often been deemed a soft-porn film because of the sexual images in the film. And sure, the asparagus images are erotic, but to say that the film is solely about sex is to miss the boat by hours.

"I thought of the asparagus as a beautiful symbol of sexuality," says Pitt. "It comes out of the ground as a phallic stalk, pointy and purple green, the essence of a beautiful masculine form. But then as summer passes it stretches tall and becomes a delicate fern, seen on roadsides tilting in the wind, the essence of the feminine-like long strands of tangled hair in the breeze."

Pitt's aim, though, was to make "a visual poem about the creative process" and take the viewer through the mind of an artist/magician as she searches for the forces that stimulate her creative existence.

"I wanted the film to mirror the way we daydream — as Jung said, 'Images are pregnant': each image leading to the next, the mind unfolding, constantly giving birth. I wanted the audience to see the film unfold as if in a daydream."

The film put Pitt firmly on the map of animation and experimental filmmaking. *Asparagus* was extremely well received for a short animation film; the film premiered at the Whitney Museum of American Art in its own miniature theatre; it was shown before David Lynch's *Eraserhead* and ran for two years in New York and then a year in Los Angeles.

Relocating to New York, Pitt found herself weary of the intense labor of animating *Asparagus* and turned her attention to paintings and constructions. "This was the heyday of the art scene in New York and most of the work I did was sold to collectors during 1979–1986 or so. I had an exhibit at the Holly Solomon Gallery in Lower Manhattan of all the artwork, transfigured, from the film — I made objects and plastic cut-outs and secret boxes and a waterfall of hundreds of tiny cut-outs of the cels. It was as though the film ran through its moving stage and then came to rest in bits and pieces in the gallery, laying down its meanings in concrete space."

With Blue headed to college, Pitt needed a steady job and returned to Harvard in 1986. She also started a new project: "I designed the sets and costumes, and created one hour of animation for a production of *The Damnation of Faust* by Hector Berlioz at the Staatsoper in Hamburg. I believe this to be the first time animation was projected for opera — we produced all the images using low-down experimental film techniques, scratching on films, animated objects under the camera, animating comic books and cut-outs in layers under glass."

Incredibly, Pitt managed to juggle the opera and teaching; she would fly frequently across the Atlantic while continuing to teach her classes. Eventually though, something would have to give, and it (or rather, she) did.

Pitt, who has suffered from depression throughout her adult life, suffered a breakdown. "I think of it as some monster inside who devours my self and pulls me down under. I constantly have had to find ways to survive and climb back out, sometimes letting it sink me for long periods and sometimes fighting by brute force through determined work."

After months of therapy, Pitt channeled her black dog demons (Winston Churchill called his depression his "black dog") into a storyboard for the film *Joy Street*.

The storyline is relatively straightforward: A suicidal woman is alone in her apartment and just as she is about to kill herself, a cartoon mouse comes to life and saves her. After she wakes up, the mouse shows her the joy and importance of the natural world. The film ends with the woman opening up her windows as the sounds of the city come to life around her.

The inspiration for the mouse came from Pitt's son, Blue. "He had given me a tiny ceramic ashtray, probably from the 1940s, with a little generic mouse sitting on it. I thought about how there must be something very pure in the essence of life — uncorrupted — existing in pure color, like the colors of the mouse and the innocence of the childlike nature of the cartoon."

Joy Street captures the extremes of manic depression: the cartoon mouse, like Voltaire's *Candide*, is eternally optimistic and hopeful; the woman is depressed, lost in a sea of futility and neurosis.

There is also an ecological aspect to the film. As the mouse shows the woman the beauty of the natural world, it becomes clear that this is something she has lost touch with by living in the city.

"I went to Mexico, Belize, and Guatemala on several different trips looking for rainforest. I painted watercolors and gouache paintings sitting under a tarp. All this for the adventure of entering nature at its most vibrant and intense in order to convey the magnificence of the rainforest. The time spent there became an awakening of my soul, and I became a parallel of the woman in the film — I myself was coming back to life through immersion in the natural world.

A restless soul, in 1998 Pitt was on the move again, this time to Los Angeles to teach at CalArts in the experimental animation program. "I've always moved around a lot — I get tired of being in one place and I like to experience different people and places, often taking my movies-in-progress with me. I need to be charged and awakened or else I fall."

After working on a series of paintings that she never showed, Pitt began work on her next film, *El Doctor* (2006).

In a small Mexican town, a bitter, ailing, alcoholic doctor stumbles onto the street towards his car. In a flash he is whisked away by two approaching medical attendants to the nearby hospital to heal a patient with holes throughout his body; the doctor sees no hope and lets the man die. As he walks back towards his car, a talking gargoyle admonishes the old doctor and tells him he'd be better off committing suicide. In his car, the doctor's heart begins to give way, and as he approaches death, the Saint of Emptiness appears to show the old man a new way of seeing life.

Tinged with elements of magic realism and Mexican culture, and told using vivid oil colors, Pitt's latest film, *El Doctor* is a dazzling, haunting and poignant evocation of a man's final moments.

Between *Joy Street* and *El Doctor*, Pitt primarily worked on paintings, some of which served as inspiration for her new film. "I did a series of paintings which pictured miraculous events taking place in Mexico. The characters I created for the paintings and the events which were pictured became the groundwork for the film."

In particular Pitt was fascinated with Mexico's affinity for the divine. "I have traveled there a lot and I know how deeply the possibility of the miraculous is imbedded in the culture — the religious and spiritual — usually a figure or image appears to someone bringing proof that the spirit world is pushing outward into the real world to bring news of a deliverance, or a message, or a religious or divine presence."

Pitt then asked her son, Blue, to write a story based on her paintings. For about six months, mother and son worked and argued on the story. "He devised a story using some of the characters which already existed and the ideas we spoke about concerning miracles and how they might be perceived and what they might mean. The frame and dialogue for animation I felt needed to be apparent but simple and not needlessly instructive in the way stories sometimes are. The images and characterizations and movement alone can carry the meaning quite well in animation. But the framework of the story which Blue wrote is the basis for the film."

Producing the film was slightly more complex: because *El*

Doctor was shot entirely on film and used full animation along with a number of characters, Pitt was forced to use a small crew. "I'm actually quite proud of the fact that everything was produced in the USA with local talent — except for animator Gérard Goulet (who worked on *The Triplets of Belleville*) who came from Montreal for six weeks to work on the film in LA."

In voicing the characters, Pitt worked with real actors for the first time. Initially she used professional Latin actors from the Los Angeles area, but quickly ran into a strange dilemma. "The actors were trying to lose their Spanish accents in order to work in LA so when I asked them to speak in a Mexican accent they seemed to revert to a stereotype — so a lot of the characters came out sounding like a Taco commercial. And just the sound and enunciation of a 'professional' seemed wrong and affected for the story."

To capture a more genuine dialect, Pitt decided to redo with recordings in Mexico. "My friend and animator Dominique Jonard found all the people and brought them to his house in Morelia. We did some rehearsing but not a lot. Some of the expressions and mistakes in English were left in the finished dialogue and added authenticity. We recorded in his living room with blankets on the walls and a portable DAT player."

While Pitt considers *El Doctor* to be her first narrative film, it would be a stretch to call the film a linear narrative. Reminiscent of contemporary Estonian animation, *El Doctor* is full of absurd situations and almost grotesque caricatures. In that sense, *El Doctor* is closer to the 'magic' realism of a writer like Gabriel García Márquez than it is to your typical classical narrative film. Pitt is also the first to admit she was challenged by the restrictions of narrative. "When you tell a story, no matter how absurd or surrealistic it is, you have to include all the necessary elements of the story so the audience can follow it. If the character has to be shown entering a door because of the script, then the challenge is to make that little animation interesting in itself and not just another 200 drawings of the character walking in the door. I had to work very hard to not feel restricted by the requirements of the story."

Another aspect of the film that breaks from a classical narrative tradition is the employment of different animation techniques to evoke a particular mood or moment in the film. "It seems that certain animation techniques because of the way they are handled and the particular characteristics of the materials involved are representative of ways of seeing or expressing. Chalk or sand by its very nature is loose, smeary, suggestive, and soft. I used sand in the scene where the doctor looks in the windshield to suggest something he was imagining, something soft and frightening appearing out of the dirt and grime of the windshield."

For the scene with Santa Esmeralda, the Saint of Emptiness, Pitt used the services of filmmaker Naomi Uman who scratched and painted directly on 35 mm film. "I asked to make her own abstract interpretation of the saint," recalls Pitt, "I told her I would accept anything she did . . . so in this way she was the actress who played the part of the saint . . . in that slow-motion way only animator actors understand."

To give the scenes with the doctor and Caballita (the woman who thinks she's a horse) a nostalgic, old-fashioned quality, Pitt animated on paper and then stained and crushed the paper. She then drew into the wrinkled images with chalk pencils.

While *El Doctor* is rife with possible interpretations, the message that comes through the cranky, cynical old doctor is that we tend to create our own strife: he sees an ugly, empty world so it remains just that. In a way, *El Doctor* is a slightly cruel film as the doctor is only shown another vision of the world as he's dying.

"I thought perhaps at the moment of death the doctor might realize that all the times he felt lousy about the world and ceased to care, he was creating the mess himself — with a different viewpoint the world was filled with possibility and beauty," notes Pitt. "Hopelessness itself creates futility, so he imagines returning to the hospital and seeing things anew. I don't think it matters whether he was able to live this way for years or only a few seconds in his mind — it still happened."

Does this moment of the divine matter in the end? Earlier in the film, the doctor says bitterly that life is nothing but a temptation, suggesting that one will never have their desires fulfilled. Is death then the satisfaction of those desires? "Well, that's an existential viewpoint, isn't it?" responds Pitt, "It doesn't matter whether the doctor was a good man or a bad man, what matters is within himself at death . . . he sees the totality, the universe. It's as if the Everything was giving him a smile and a nod and letting him dream away dressed in his beautiful Mariachi suit with the light blue tie and riding his favourite imagined horse, and carrying his lovely girl from long ago who still wears her Mexican dress and braids her hair in the traditional style and holds him tightly as their footsteps slip away." In the end, the doctor's life amounts to little more than a moment, but what a moment it is.

"Is that all there is?" chimed Peggy Lee once upon a time.

That is all, and that ain't bad (don't matter if it is).

"Death," adds Pitt, "is not so frightening when one believes that which we do not know clearly is larger than our small lives and therefore this large 'other' will embrace our deaths with meaning."

With *El Doctor* in the can, Pitt isn't entirely sure when she will make another film. It seems as though she has grown somewhat frustrated with the limited rewards that come from, especially in Pitt's case, the tedious and lengthy process of making independent animation. "The understanding and appreciation of experimental animation is so small and remote compared to famous writers, composers, painters, and others in artistic fields. Perhaps it is the lack of physical substance (as in paintings and sculptures) which makes the ephemeral time-based works of animation artists seem less 'valuable'. Perhaps one cannot wish for more when making simple magic."

Figure 15.1 Don Hertzfeldt

Figure 15.2 *Rejected*

Figure 15.3 *I Am So Proud of You*

CHAPTER 15

In the Dust and Moonlight of Don Hertzfeldt

The thought of Don Hertzfeldt not being able to make films scares me. Hertzfeldt's characters (those in *Genre* and *Ah, L'Amour*) are anguished souls simply longing to be accepted, to be loved, to be. The fierce frankness of these violent emotions is legitimate. Hertzfeldt's work shares a strange sort of kinship with the writing of Hubert Selby Jr. (*The Room* and *Requiem for a Dream*) in its unearthing of the rage of existence and madness that creeps and crawls within us. There are times when it howls to be unleashed upon the world, and times when it spurts out in a small shout, a dirty look or a middle finger. Some do it in a bar; some do it on a hockey rink; Don Hertzfeldt does it on a piece of paper.

Hertzfeldt has been drawing since he smashed Lacan's mirror and first took up image-making when he was 15. "I got a VHS camera that could shoot a hackneyed version of single frames, so I was able to teach myself some basics through high school."

After high school, Hertzfeldt went to the University of California, Santa Barbara. "I wanted to be Stanley Kubrick like everyone else, but live action was very expensive to tackle, this was back when it was all 16 mm. but I realized I had unlimited, unsupervised access to their animation camera."

For the next four years at university, Hertzfeldt made four animation films. "I carried on there with animating all my student films because you didn't need to buy as much film; and it was possible to make a movie that way with a really minimal crew."

Oddly enough, Hertzfeldt went to film school but ended up teaching himself animation; still, he maintains that school was very important to his development. "I'm not sure if my movies would have been very good if I hadn't gone to film school. Studying the guts and language of movies, the history and theory, focuses your flailing about into clearer ideas on the screen. You can't make a movie if you only understand how to draw."

Ah L'Amour (1995) was Hertzfeldt's debut as an animator. Hertzfeldt's primitive and minimal black-and-white style is already recognizable in this short gag film about a guy whose attempts to pick up a girl are met with continual violence. It's not until the guy says that he has money that the girl finally accepts him.

Despite, or perhaps because of, the film's misogynistic leanings, *Ah L'Amour* was an instant cult hit. The film was scooped up by the Spike and Mike's traveling festival and screened across the US where it found sympathetic fans in horny young American men who knew all too well the bitter taste of rejection.

The success of *Ah L'Amour* started a trend that Hertzfeldt has maintained throughout his career: each successive short film is funded from money made from the previous film. "I've never lost money on a film and have never had to have a traditional job, never had to do commercial work out of necessity."

A major influence on Hertzfeldt's approach to animation was Bill Plympton, arguably the most successful and famous independent animator in the world. "I saw Bill's first few shorts when I was 12 or 13 and yeah, it was invaluable to realize there was somebody out there who's regularly able to do this for a living, and do it on his own terms (and who doesn't draw backgrounds either!). For a long time I think he's been a guy that a lot of people have pointed to and said, 'well if he's figured out a way to do this, maybe I can too.'"

L'Amour funded *Genre* (1996), Hertzfeldt's weakest film, which follows a long tired line of self-reflexive films (e.g. *Duck Amuck*, *Koko the Clown*) that depict a battle between the animator and his character. This time the character (a rabbit) is tossed into various genre films. Although there are a few funny gags (for example, when the rabbit finds himself in a porn film with his buddy), the film quickly runs out of steam. "I was 19 when we made it, my second year in school, and was still following this kind of setup-gag-punchline formula. But, it was fun to make and at the time I was just excited to learn how to pull something off as long as 5 minutes."

Lily and Jim (1997), a he-said/she-said story about a man and woman out on a blind date, represents another step forward in Hertzfeldt's career. The minimal drawing style remains, but the drawings and storyline are more structured and fleshed out, and Hertzfeldt's film school influence is also apparent. With echoes of *Annie Hall*, *Lily and Jim* is divided into two segments: in the black-and-white segment, each character talks about the date to an off-camera interviewer (or maybe it's "us" the audience), while the actual date segment is shot with color.

The bulk of the film is slow and awkward — some of this could be pinned on a young, inexperienced artist, but it also cleverly captures the often painful and tedious experience of dating. Throughout the date, the couple struggle to come up with something to talk about. At one point, à la *Annie Hall*, thought bubbles reveal what they're really thinking during their conversation. In the end, despite having a relatively lame date (aside from Jim having to be taken to the hospital after he suffers an allergic reaction to coffee), Lily and Jim tell the audience/interviewer that they want to see each other again; however, their insecurities and false bravado ensure that it never happens. They remain alone.

Lily and Jim revealed to audiences that there was more to Hertzfeldt than just infantile gag films, and Hertzfeldt remains happy with the film. "This was a real lucky match of casting and on-the-fly writing. I had the actors improvise a lot and they performed some miracles that we cleverly blended into my script. Once that was all locked in and the dialogue was handed off to me in giant stacks of exposure sheets, it was one of the more boring projects to sit down with and draw every night." In the end, Hertzfeldt figures he drew over ten thousand drawings for the films! "I still have no idea how I was able to fully animate a 12-minute movie while going to school full time."

Billy's Balloon marked a return to Hertzfeldt's earlier gag films, but this time with a surrealist twist guaranteed to make every precious parent cringe: a young boy sits happily with a toy and red balloon, when suddenly the balloon comes alive and starts beating the shit out of the boy. This continues for the entire film until we see other kids being tortured by their balloons.

Billy's Balloon shouldn't work, but it does because, like an Ol' Dirty Bastard song, the violence is so utterly absurd that you can't help but laugh.

After the long process of making *Lily and Jim*, Hertzfeldt was happy to produce a relatively fast and light film. "I remember it partially coming out of a dream about a boy in a field who begins to fly. I think I produced it relatively fast, maybe in nine months. I originally had a dumb sort of punchline gag for the ending and quickly decided against it. Otherwise I think it was pretty straightforward and didn't change drastically from start to finish.

With a dash of Monty Python and a whole lot of Hertzfeldt weirdness, the Oscar-nominated *Rejected* is a series of fake and very absurd rejected IDs and commercials. While the gruesome gags echo *Billy's Balloon* and *Ah L'amour*, the freewheeling, experimental structure ultimately points towards some of the structures and themes of Hertzfeldt's later films. *Rejected* is less a series of ultra-violent gags then it is about a creator suffering a mental meltdown (at one point the title card reads: "Don's clear and steady downhill state continued. Soon he was completing commercial segments entirely with his left hand"). As the film progresses, the structure and logic become increasingly fragmented; humor and absurdity give way to fear as the characters flee their creator. The film ends with the artist's papers and characters being destroyed.

Not surprisingly, the creative approach to *Rejected* was almost entirely experimental. "Maybe this was my Sgt. Pepper phase. Chunks were swapped around, reanimated, dialogue scenes were animated without the dialogue having been written yet . . . it was also my first time screwing around with in-camera effects. The sound work played the biggest role, with last-minute improvisations, seemingly every other line being played backwards, more rewrites. I think almost every scene was thrown up against the wall, re-recorded and torn back down again a number of different ways. It was a very strange but exciting way to work."

With *The Meaning of Life* (2005), Hertzfeldt's films entered ambitious new territory. The films became more epic in scope and experimental in tone and the violence and humor of the earlier films are secondary outcomes for characters struggling with existence, identity and madness.

The Meaning of Life is unlike anything Hertzfeldt has made before: a personal, playful and poignant take on life. Starting with the evolution of man, Hertzfeldt takes us through a world of babbling humans, aliens and, finally, an alien father and son. The creatures and their worlds come and go, but the thing that remains constant is the beauty and mystery of the stars and suns of the universe. The ultimate irony is that the eternal human question, "what is the meaning of life" cannot be answered in words.

The Meaning of Life took Hertzfeldt almost four years to make. "I didn't write the ending until I was two years into animating it, but other than that I think there was relatively little that changed from the first ideas to the finished product. I was happy with the finished movie but not having a pliable structure that I could play around with and rewrite and shape as I went made it frustrating and very difficult to work on. Life's too short to lock yourself up for that long working on something called *The Meaning of Life*."

Everything Will Be Ok (2006) and *I Am So Proud of You* (2008) are two chapters from the same story (a third chapter is forthcoming). Both films star Bill, a man with some serious personality disorder issues. Bill sees the world through small moving holes, and his many, fragmented social encounters reveal a man who is paranoid, obsessed, anxious and generally unable to connect with the world around him (even if he does occasionally see the beauty of it). He becomes increasingly fragmented and disorientated — death and nightmares haunt him. Finally, Bill goes to see a doctor, but medication only makes Bill's perspective increasingly disorientated, nightmarish and illogical. Reality and fantasy blur to the point where Bill collapses into a nervous breakdown. On the brink of death, Bill eventually recovers. Eventually he returns to his normal life. Through all his pain, Bill never complains. He just goes on.

Everything Will Be Ok is a stunning piece of work that manages to offer an insightful, funny and painful perspective of a fucked-up human being, no longer able to make sense of or engage with the world around him. Hertzfeldt's ingenious use of moving holes, reminiscent of silent films, puts the viewer right behind the eyes of poor troubled Bill.

Hertzfeldt says that the roots of the trilogy start with a WWII story he once read about Nazis invading a town. "The protagonist is in a large group of people who are being marched through the city and across a bridge where they're going to be shot. This man has lived in this town his entire life, but as he's being marched off to die he notices details in the cobblestone streets he's never seen before. He sees new things in the faces of the people around him, people he's known for years. The air smells different. The currents in the river look strange and new. Suddenly he's seeing the world around him for the first time through these new lenses and it's disorienting and beautiful. It takes a horrible event sometimes to grab you by the shoulders and shake you, to wake you up."

When *I Am So Proud of You* traveled North America in 2008, the following blurb served as promotion fodder:

". . . a fucking masterpiece. I can't even begin to articulate my thoughts about the film but it just gave me shivers and I wasn't able to attend the party after the screening. Just had to be alone. It had this effect on a number of other people here too . . . stunning, beautiful, tragic, absurd work."

I wrote those words to Hertzfeldt in an e-mail a few hours after watching *I Am So Proud of You*. No animation film has had such a potent and conflicting impact on me; the experience reminded me of reading the first chapter of William Faulkner's classic novel, *The Sound and the Fury*. I found the chapter infuriating, funny, confusing and exhausting, and it was only near the end of the chapter that I realized the story was being told by a character with some serious mental defects. The experience of watching *I Am So Proud* is similar. It's a work that takes us out of our experience; we walk in the shoes of a conflicted and sick man as he drifts through the fragments of his past and present.

"Bill's been slapped in the face with something horrible and the world is looking very different to him, sad and beautiful. It's somebody facing death who hasn't really lived yet. The routine things he's used to doing are suddenly completely redundant. You begin to see how death enriches life and gives everything its meaning. It's the people who drift around wasting their time, weirdly assuming they're going to live forever that are the depressing ones, to me at least."

As different as Hertzfeldt's films are, the underlying themes of madness, depression and fractured identity run through his entire body of work. "It's something I've always been interested in. I love comedy of course; some of these films exist for no other reason than to make you laugh. On other projects it's used more like the sugar you give to make the medicine go down easier. A friend once pointed out that the chain between all the films, beneath the comedy, is 'quiet dread' . . . I've been called an existentialist more than once, in which case madness is probably just a character's symptom."

While Hertzfeldt is more interested in storytelling than in "dumping emotional baggage" on viewers, he admits that process of animating the films can be therapeutic. "You sit all alone for months and patiently build something bigger out of thousands of almost invisible movements (doesn't that sound kind of tai chi or something?) and it's very good to be forced to be alone with your thoughts, which animation requires in spades. Too few people are truly alone with their thoughts anymore."

Hertzfeldt's films are also remarkable because of the way they're made: aside from editing and sound mixing his films digitally, Hertzfeldt uses no computers. With technology having advanced so far that animators can make quality work much quicker than at any other time in animation history, Hertzfeldt is content to take his time. In fact he contends that the "old" way is not necessarily difficult.

"Many people like to assume that because I shoot on film and animate on paper I must be doing things 'the hard way', when really my last four movies would've been visually impossible to produce digitally, if not extremely difficult and much more expensive. There are some things traditional cameras do much better than computers, and vice versa."

Given the increased length of his films it's surprising to hear that Hertzfeldt isn't that interested in making a feature film. "No, features are a horse of a different color. If I were to tackle a feature alone it would probably take 20 years. I'd need a studio's help and financial backing, like I'm putting together now for TV — but nobody in those feature film positions are really interested in doing hand-drawn animation anymore."

Hertzfeldt is succeeding just fine making short films: he has total creative freedom and manages to make a living off them — few short film animators can say that. "Why bang my head against the wall trying to conjure up something to please a studio? Just last week I read a great Martin Scorsese quote: 'don't make the movies you *can* make, make the movies you *want* to make.'"

And live the life you want to live.

Figure 16.1   Chris Shepherd

Figure 16.2   *Dad's Dead*

Figure 16.3   Pete

CHAPTER 16

Chris Shepherd

Who He Is and What He Wants

British animator Chris Shepherd has done pretty well for himself. Not only is he the successful partner of the British animation studio, Slinky Pictures, he's also directed three of the most striking and original animation works of the last decade: the deliciously dark *Dad's Dead* (2003); *Who I Am and What I Want* (2005), a hilarious and disturbing scribble film about a fucked-up guy in denial named Pete — made in collaboration with Scottish artist, David Shrigley — and *Silence is Golden* (2006), a live-action/animation hybrid about a young boy, his boozer mom and their crazy old neighbor.

The Liverpool born Shepherd studied Foundation Art at Liverpool Polytechnic, and then studied animation at West Surrey College of Art and Design. After graduating in 1992, he served as studio manager at Speedy Films before starting up his own company, Polkadot Productions, three years later.

Through Polkadot, Shepherd created a number of commissioned films along with two award-winning shorts for TV: *The Broken Jaw* (1997) and the hilarious minimalist anti-animation *Stare Out Final* (1998) for the BBC show *Big Train*.

In 2000 he became the co-founder of production company Slinky Pictures, with producer Maria Manton. Under the Slinky banner, Shepherd managed to create an ideal situation allowing him to do both commissioned and personal projects. The first of Shepherd's indie films was the powerful *Dad's Dead*.

In *Dad's Dead*, memories of a troubled childhood friend named Johnno lead an unnamed man to reexamine his past. Piecing together the fragments, the man goes from idolizing his adventurous, charming friend to loathing his violent and messed-up mate. In a surprising and creepy ending, the unnamed man (who might actually be Johnno) pays the price for their friendship.

Dad's Dead is a rarity in animation. Here's an aggressive, urban film telling real stories about flawed people living a dirty, vile existence: Shepherd's film is planets away from Pixar. The fusion of live-action and animation gives the film a unique, disturbing look, capturing the distorted nature of memory.

Although Shepherd wrote the script for *Dad's Dead* in 1999 and recorded Ian Hart's narration the same year, he wasn't able to start production on the film immediately. "I didn't have any money to make it then, so put the disc in my cupboard for ages and went off and did other things. To be honest I didn't think it would be something anybody would want to commission, because it's quite dark, but I always had a burning desire to make the film."

Shepherd finally received funding in 2002. "The shoot was quite unusual because I tried to build it up like it was a painting — I did six shoots over the space of a year. I'd shoot one scene, cut it, combine it with some animation, then go away, think about it, and then shoot another scene. I kept building it up in layers."

Prior to *Dad's Dead*, Shepherd had primarily made commercials along with some drawn animation. With this film he wanted to capture the emotional resonance of live-action and merge it with animation. "I suppose I'd seen lots of animation films that were always about quite surreal things or poetic stories, but I never really related to them. They didn't reflect where I grew up, and they didn't reflect my Liverpool, so I wanted to do a film that was more about my background but have these aspects of poetry and style in them. Essentially the story is all fiction though, because I think if I met somebody like the character of Johnno, I wouldn't live to tell the tale!"

People were shocked after seeing the premiere of *Dad's Dead* — in fact, so was Shepherd. "It's very aggressive and it really beats you up. I remember the first screening. I had no idea what people were going to think of it. We only screened it once and people were just shocked, stunned . . . they didn't expect me to do something so dark. People I'd known for years just didn't know what to say to me afterwards! It was such a departure from the other stuff I'd done. It's funny when I think back, but you've got to try and do different things because that's what it's all about, isn't it?"

The idea of collaborating with Scottish artist David Shrigley began in 1998 when Shepherd was working on the British sketch TV show *Big Train*. "I read a book by David called "*Why we got the Sack from the Museum,*" recalls Shepherd. "It reminded me of school. I got in trouble one time for drawing all over the walls of the sixth-form common room. These drawings did not get me top marks. Obscenity was not in fashion then. The headmaster was not happy, he said I'd blown my chances of being the head boy and I was heading straight to the chicken giblet factory to be a packer when I left school. Thank you sir. David's book spoke volumes to me, the rawness of it took me back to those school days." Shepherd then asked Shrigley if he wanted to collaborate on an animation film; Shrigley agreed and then the two artists spent the next five years talking about it. Finally, Shrigley showed Shepherd his book, *Who I Am and What I Want*, and both agreed that the story should be the basis for the film.

Shrigley, though, didn't just send his story to Shepherd and be done with it: the two collaborated on every aspect of the production. "We bounced the script between us via e-mail trying to make the book work as a film. We decided early on that we would use a voice over and not have written text in picture. Once we were happy with the script I did a rough animatic and from that David drew a kit of parts for me: a page of street furniture, trees, people, etc. From this we built a world for Pete to live in. So a lot of what you see in the film is David's original drawings."

Complementing Shrigley's perfectly primitive drawings is the narration of actor Kevin Eldon. Eldon's machine-gun pace and smart-ass tone — not to forget Shrigley's sharp, sparse text — are key to the film's success. "David was originally going to do the voice himself," says Shepherd. "I kept thinking back to when I was on *Big Train* and a sketch where Kevin Eldon played the Devil working in an office where Jesus was his boss. His character was quite belligerent. His voice was in my head when we read through the script. We both thought Kevin was the right choice. It was clever the way Kevin played Pete. An educated man in a state of total denial. Like he's holding in all of the madness. An academic on the verge of a mental breakdown. You could have played him as the crazy man, but we both knew that could have been a big mistake."

Silence is Golden emerged from a very different background.

"I tend to be a bit of a magpie, I use elements from my youth in my work, but I mix everything up, stories people tell me, things I've overheard on the bus. I'm a very nosy person. I don't wear a watch as I figure I then have an excuse to look into people's living rooms. I've seen all kinds of things that way."

While *Silence is Golden* is predominantly live-action, the animation plays a pivotal role in the film as a stand-in for young Billy's lively imagination. "I like people and the real world. I also like imagining stuff in the context of everyday settings. So it's natural for me to mix live action with animation. In *Silence*, it's all Billy's about fantasies. The world inside Billy's head was like a seventies episode of *Doctor Who*, although maybe it's a bit darker than what you might see on the telly. In contrast to *Dad's Dead* I wanted all of the fantasies to be realistic, that's the way I imagine things. We went to great lengths to achieve this. For example, the scene where the Moonies get fried, I got hold of a flame thrower that could fire flame 30 feet and filmed all of the flames the way you see them in the film. A lot of things were blown up in that shoot."

Animation festivals are notoriously anal-rententive about hybrid films but that doesn't worry Shepherd. "It's a bit early to tell what will happen with *Silence* yet. Films tend to find their own audiences. When I made *Dad's Dead* I figured everyone would hate it, but to my surprise both live-action and animation festivals went for it. *Who I Am* appeals to a different bunch again. *Silence Is Golden* will no doubt attract a different bunch again."

All three of Shepherd's films have been dark portraits of a fucked-up side of humanity. These are subjects that few animators are willing to tackle; this is changing to a degree, but for the most part, animators have wanted to make "precious" films about the beauty of life. That's not a bad thing, but you can't see the light without the dark. We live in a world that is increasingly fragmented, isolated and discontent; is animation adequately reflecting this state or living in a rose-colored hippie world filled with good talk?

"Sometimes bad things can be beautiful or poetic," says Shepherd. "It's one thing to try ignoring bad stuff, but don't we all want to know why it happens? What makes people tick? I figure that's what writers like Hubert Selby Jr. do. They make us understand the reason for the bad things. Those stories are quite often the ones that interest me. The main thing for me is that I try not to judge the characters in my films; I like to show the story and let the audience decide if they are good or bad. It's not my place to judge people."

Who I Am, in particular, is a savage excavation of a seemingly decent, normal guy that certainly resembles some of the characters of the very fine writings of Hubert Selby Jr. (notably *The Room*, probably his most disturbing book). Shepherd's films fall in the ranks of other animated poets of the darkness, like Andreas Hykade, J J Villard, Phil Mulloy and Michèle Cournoyer: they take us to worlds we don't want to, but *need* to, see.

Figure 17.1   Run Wrake

Figure 17.2   *Rabbit*

Figure 17.3   *The Control Master*

CHAPTER 17

Run Wrake Ain't No Meathead

Watching a Run Wrake animation is like tapping into the unconscious mind of some extremely high musical genius. Utilizing bold line drawings, Wrake connects a barrage of imagery from diverse media and loops it with a brilliant sense of rhythm. It's not surprising that this Royal College of Art graduate has found success interpreting inventive musical artists such as Gang of Four, Howie B, Oasis and Future Sound of London. In addition he's done MTV IDs, commercials, illustrative work and visuals for U2's PopMart and Vertigo tours. Most recently Wrake has taken on narratives with the highly successful short films *Rabbit* (2006) and *The Control Master* (2008).

Wrake was born John Wrake in the Republic of Yemen in 1965. His father was an army chaplain, and the Wrake family moved to Sussex, England when Run (he earned the nickname just after relocating) turned 11.

Run Wrake's earliest — or at least most memorable — encounter with animation came in the 1970s. Wrake recalls seeing an episode of the UK TV show *The Old Grey Whistle Test*. "They used to play album tracks cut to grainy old black and white animation that looked like the Fleischer Brothers." Animation had entered Wrake's consciousness, but it would be a while before he seriously considered it as a career. Most of Wrake's days were spent fishing, digging up old bottles and collecting material — little did he know that his hoarding would eventually inspire his art. "Found material has always been a big part of my work. I can't pass a junk shop without stopping."

After secondary school, Wrake signed up for graphics at the Chelsea College of Art and Design. Although Wrake was heavily influenced by Dada graphics, he says that music was his primary artistic inspiration. "I was doing graphic design but buying and listening to a lot of music, and animation was a way of combining the two." The idea of merging music and animation was inspired by a foundation class taught by an artist who had made a video for the band Art of Noise. "That was the real catalyst. It was very collage-y — cut very tightly to the beat — and it just really appealed to me, that combination of sound and image tightly synchronized, so that was the real turning point."

At Chelsea, Wrake made the student film *Interest* (1987). Wrake's love of beats and morphing imagery is already present in this fast-moving groove feast. "I just bought a pile of 10p offcut pads from a printers, and made it up as I went along, the bleed through the paper from the marker pens used providing alternative to a lightbox. The track was added after."

After graduating from Chelsea, Wrake went on to the prestigious Royal College of Art (RCA). The experience at RCA was a pivotal one. "Chelsea had no facilities really, all the films I made there were shot and edited in camera, super 8 and 16 mm, and then telecine'd to tape and music added. So, most importantly RCA introduced me to the picture-sync machine, enabling the planning of picture and its relation to a broken down soundtrack. I learned how you can break down sound and create a map of the soundtrack so you knew exactly which frame the beat would hit, and that was the real revelation for me — that you could create images to perfectly replicate the music."

Wrake's graduation film, *Anyway* (1990), follows the same path as *Interest* but the images are more vibrant and alive. Crowded frames of surreal images jump through the frames. "*Anyway* started with the soundtrack, put together using the record and pause buttons on a Teac 4-track tape recorder and my record collection. The animation was created again sans storyboard, but with the broken-down track as a guideline. Hand-drawn, cut and paste artwork shot and cut on 16 mm film."

Aside from the Dada influence, collage art and the work of Keith Haring inspired Wrake's early films. Wrake loved the power and vibrancy of these artists: "It just leaps out at you off the wall. That's what I like. Things that leap out and kick you in the teeth."

Following his graduation from RCA, Wrake landed a gig doing title sequences for a series of film documentaries produced by Jonathan Ross. He then made the music promo *Cadillac* (1991) for Gang of Four before creating one of his masterworks to date, *Jukebox* (1994).

Jukebox is a stream-of-consciousness masterpiece littered with wild beats (including bits of Curtis Mayfield's *Move on Up*) and array of looped, drawn and collage imagery that ranges from the surreal to pop culture. Watching *Jukebox* is a bit like spending the night in a dance club: it's an upbeat, fractured ride through a world of paranoia, fear and joy.

One of the most striking images from *Jukebox* is the meathead character — who appears in many of Wrake's films. "The meathead thing started as the metaphor for the fear of someone being confronted with a dog, but has become more about the fact that we're all just living meat beneath our labels."

The initial idea behind *Jukebox* came from a W. H. Auden poem, "As I came out one evening". After two years of "blood, sweat and tears," Wrake got bored with the project and abandoned it in favour of a more off-the-cuff approach.

Jukebox was well received on the festival circuit, but the most significant viewer was musician Howie B. "Howie saw *Jukebox* and we went out for dinner and hit it off. The appeal was the similarity in the creation of our respective work at the time namely loops." The meeting led to a string of collaborations between the two artists including Wrake's next short film, *Music For Babies* (1996).

Commissioned by Howie B and Polydor Records, *Music for Babies* follows the visually explosive *Jukebox* with a narrative loosely based on the experience of being a new father. Beginning with the birth of a child and flowing into a series of images containing child and parent motifs, the rhythm of the film is more subdued here than in *Jukebox*. Fear and paranoia are replaced by bouts of calmness, restlessness and repetition. Image and music are so tightly interwoven that it seems impossible for one to exist without the other.

With a signature style in place, Wrake found ample work over the next decade. Aside from illustrations and various commercials, Wrake made videos for Howie B (*Butt Meat, Maniac Melody*), Robbie Robertson (*Take Your Partner by The Hand*) and Future Sound of London (*We Have Explosive*). While Wrake enjoys the creative challenge of working with clients, he admits that the experience can be creatively frustrating. "In an ideal world I would have the money to just make independent films, but alas I need to make a living.

One of Wrake's most unique jobs was creating visuals for U2's PopMart tour in 1997. "It was a great job, great experience all round. Came about through Catherine Owens, who was overseeing the production of visual material for Popmart, getting reels from RCA and giving me a call. Willie Williams, show designer, had a fairly clear idea of which Lichtenstein paintings he wanted animated, though not how. In some ways creating stuff for live performance goes right back to my earliest work in that there are no definite sync points, as the way the song is performed differs each time, so you have the element of chance much more than in a promo." U2 was so pleased with Wrake's work they brought him back to do visuals during their Vertigo tour in 2005.

In 2006, Wrake's animation took a drastic turn away from freewheeling, abstract imagery towards work that was more structured and narrative driven.

You know those Dick and Jane books, eh? They tell the adventures of two little kids and their dog Spot (*See Spot Run*). They live in a carefree and innocent world. The illustrations, like the text, are clear and simple. I don't recall reading them as a kid, but my son Jarvis certainly read them — might have been the first book he read. Typically (of my juvenile leftovers anyway), I inevitably began to think dirty, dark thoughts about these puritanical little darlings: "See Jane do Dick" and assorted clever stuff like that.

Across the blue, in England, a chap named Geoffrey Higham was a book illustrator who created similar books. Wrake, perhaps fuelled by the same unsavoury imaginings I had about Dick and Jane, decided to take Higham's original illustrations and turn them into a bizarre little film called *Rabbit.*

From appearance of the first word, "muff," we know we're in for something different. A Dick-and-Jane-type boy and girl kill a rabbit running in a field. They take the dead animal home, cut it up, and out pops a mysterious little idol. Seems that this creepy little freak can change flies into diamonds, so as they dream of becoming wealthy, the devilish little duo decide to exploit the situation and entice the idol to create more diamonds. When their greed goes too far, however, the boy and girl pay the price for their wicked ways (I won't spoil the delicious ending).

The story alone is nothing special, but combined with Wrake's clever use of Higham's original illustrations — complete with accompanying text to describe every image in the film (just in case you want to brush up on your reading) — *Rabbit* becomes a disturbing and sinister atmosphere that recalls David Lynch's *Blue Velvet.*

The roots of the film go back a couple of years: while setting up a new studio, Wrake stumbled across some abandoned items at the bottom of a drawer. "In the early eighties, I found a few dusty old envelopes containing a selection of fifties educational stickers in a junk shop. They settled themselves at the bottom of a drawer for 20 years, until I rediscovered them."

The idea for the film came from this collection of educational stickers created by Higham. "They have an innocence about them, partly because they are for children, but also because they come from a seemingly more innocent time, and I thought it would be interesting to present them as they have perhaps grown up, in an age where greed is often regarded as a virtue."

Wrake laid out the hundreds of illustrations in order to find a potential storyline. He found the inspiration in the "I is for the idol" sticker. "I thought that it was an odd choice to illustrate the letter 'i' for children, it stuck out from the rest. I knew that I wanted to incorporate some drawn morphs into the film, and this led to the idea of the idol having magical powers of transformation. I was a big fan of the Moomins (books by Tove Jansson) as a child, and loved the Hobgoblin's hat, which changed any object placed in it into something else, I think this may have been an influence also."

With the concept in place, Wrake then scanned the original illustrations into Photoshop and layered them into movable body parts, and animated in Adobe After Effects CS4.

We love to mock and scorn old educational films (in the mid-1990s I stumbled upon a horde of old 16 mm educational films dealing with proper social etiquette, work behaviour, etc. . . . I screened the films at a local bar and people loved them in this ironic, detached way) or innocent creations like Dick and Jane. Is it because we've become a cynical generation that has lost touch with rituals or just a symptom — whatever the era — of becoming an adult and losing that childhood innocence and naivety?

"I guess in every age," says Wrake, "what has gone before is treated as somehow less important/relevant than the present culture by the majority of people. Often true, so much culture is intrinsically linked to the events and mindset of its time. However, the human condition never really changes at its most fundamental level, which is why the paintings of the Renaissance or the music of Mozart are as relevant today as they were in their time.

We may think we are more advanced because we have cars

with satellite navigation computers and endless TV channels, but emotionally we are the same as ever."

Wrake, though, was less interested in scorning the past than in placing them within the realities of the modern world. "In an age where the slow exhaustion of resources by an ever expanding population is becoming an inevitable reality, the simple nature of the illustrations and their content, and the world they represent, don't seem so foolish.

The effectiveness and uniqueness of *Rabbit* stems from the clash between Higham's righteous dreamworld and the truth of human nature; we know that such a virtuous world does not and cannot exist.

We laugh, but it's really quite sad.

Rabbit was a massive success on the animation and festival circuit. Encouraged by the response, Wrake took another stab at narrative and found images. Commissioned by Veer to promote their CSA Images collection of vintage stock art, Wrake made the quirky sci-fi parody *The Control Master* (2008).

Extending the themes of *Rabbit,* Wrake takes a variety of innocent-looking art images from around the 1940s and 1950s and turns them on their head. Halftone City is an innocent and peaceful American town, and its inhabitants are comfortably living the good life of the American dream. What the citizens of Halftone don't realize is that Dorothy Gayne, a mild-mannered blonde, secretly protects the citizens of Halftone from evildoers. When the evil Doctor Moire gets his mitts on a powerful new gun and shrinks Dorothy, what will the people of Halftone do? Who will save them from Doctor Moire?

While *The Control Master* is original, engaging and entertaining, the film lacks the often brilliant, playful absurdity of Wrake's earlier works. The majority of Wrake's films demand repeat viewings: each experience offers a new revelation. This isn't the case with *The Control Master*. Like a good piece of Hubba Bubba, *Control Master* is momentarily sweet and sumptuous, but then the flavour wears out, the gum is tossed, the moment forgotten.

Currently, Wrake is taking yet another new road. Not only did he recently become a father for the first time, but he's also venturing into more commercial territory: "I'm doing a short piece for Disney, attempting to encourage pre-school children to save water, or more likely, bother their parents!"

If we're lucky, kids around the world will get their first taste of meathead.

Figure 18.1   Mait Laas

Figure 18.2   *Päevavalgus*

Figure 18.3   *The Way to Nirvana*

CHAPTER 18

The Dreamworlds of Mait Laas

"For me, it's stupid to talk about yourself," says Mait Laas (who proceeds to do so anyway), "I was happy to grow up with my parents because they took very good care of me. I was their second child. The first one unfortunately died and I think they took extra care of me after that." The family was close and they traveled a lot. Laas's father worked in a factory as an engineer; his job was to think up new technologies. His mother worked as a civil servant and, despite the stagnant job, she seems to be the root of her son's artistic aspirations. "She's always looking at the clouds and she wants to know what we see. She was always thinking about things in a different way."

"I was really bad at first," notes Laas. I insisted on sports over arts because I wanted to be like the other boys, but I preferred being up in the trees with the apples." One day Laas was even beaten for refusing to write the number six in a normal way.

And, like Estonian puppet animator pioneer, Heino Pars, Laas wanted to be a beekeeper. "I was sure I would go to the country and be a beekeeper, but my teacher said, 'the boys will beat you.' She wanted me to go the art class." A further problem was that Laas was not a Komsomol — a member of the Communist Youth Organization that everyone had to belong to. At the time, everyone had to have a high level of education and be a Komsomol.

Laas's refusal to conform evolved out of respect for his rebellious grandfather. His grandfather, who was a wealthy man, had fought with the Germans against the Russians and for that he was sent, along with his family (including his newborn daughter, Laas's mother) to Siberia. All but the grandfather returned. "I was proud of them," says Laas.

At one point, Laas was called before the KGB. They wanted to set him on the right path with a little show-and-tell about dissidents: "They tried to scare me with pictures of other punks and how they could be killed or put in prison. They wanted me to be with their church . . . I wanted to follow my father."

As the 1980s roared on and the Estonian Republic became more vocal about reclaiming independence, Laas was one of the many youths swept up by the romantic patriotism of the times: "It was the best time for youth because we had something to believe in."

Laas made out okay — he was part of a semi-professional folk dance troupe and had many opportunities to travel to some interesting places: France, Germany and Chernobyl. "When I was 14 we went to Chernobyl on some empty train. This was one year after the accident. Everything was empty. It was like Tarkovsky's 'zone' [from Tarkovsky's film *Stalker*]." The troupe had been sent there to dance for the workers, to cheer them up. They were only about 40 km from the site. "It was a paradox. They would say no you can't go there, but if you don't go there we will stop the folk dance tours." While Laas escaped harm during his brief visit, an uncle, who lived in Chernobyl, died of radiation poisoning. "He didn't know anything at the time. He just lived there and no one told him anything. He was sent there to work. People were optimistic because they didn't know anything. It was a form of genocide."

Finally, Laas made it to art school. Times had changed, people forgot; Laas studied art teaching, focusing on general art and a bit of drama. For his graduation project, Laas wanted to use animation because "it mixed all sorts of arts together." He brought a story he'd written to Nukufilm, met with Riho Unt and Hardi Volmer, explained his idea and was shown the camera and told to "go ahead." "I had no idea what I had to do. Someone put film in the camera, Arvo Nuut told me what to do, and I did it and this was my graduation project." The film, *Ja õitseski* (*And It Bloomed*, 1993), was a paint-on-glass piece about seeds that wish to become flowers.

Following his graduation, Laas studied music therapy and then traveled to Vienna where he studied art philosophy and visual media. When Laas returned, he brought a second story to Nukufilm, but before his script was accepted, Laas was called on to help Hardi Volmer with a film called *Keegi Veel* (*Somebody Else*, 1996): "Hardi had started a film and he was also busy with a feature. He needed some help." It was hard for Laas, who was a little starstruck, to work with the well-known Volmer. "I would do these things and then he would come, say little, change everything and go. I didn't know what we were doing really or where we were going. But it was a good starting point for me. I felt a lot of responsibility . . . I was afraid but he let me do my own things."

After *Somebody Else*, Laas was given the opportunity to make his own film, *Päevavalgus* (*Daylight*, 1997). From a technical standpoint, *Daylight* is remarkable. Its mixed-media technique of photocopied heads (which in close-up look like the dirty, grainy expressionist faces of Eisenstein's staircase victims in *The Battleship Potemkin*) on 3-D wire bodies is eye-catching and innovative. Conceptually, *Daylight* is almost an anomaly for a young artist — it's actually a positive film. There is no loud rebellious scream against society, just an innocent, hippie-induced call for love, light and peace.

The film is set in a neighborhood block. A group of boys play; they are dark, feckless and full of pent up rage — they destroy for no reason. A boy with a flower and a smile arrives. The cynical boys frown upon him. Meanwhile, in the background, a man and a woman (the boy's parents?) abuse one another with screams and fists. Eventually, light overwhelms the neighborhood block and brightens life. But is this just the dream of a sick boy in a hospital? The structure is not altogether clear and it hinders a thorough understanding of the film. But what is clear is Laas's criticism of those dark forces of violence, cynicism and anger.

"I'm a positive person, always on the side of sunshine. I don't like these dark people who are always in the dark, living with their computers. I had the feeling that I had to make this film to help these dark people, to give them back the energy that they had lost."

Teekond Nirvaanasse (*Way To Nirvana*, 2000) is about a young man who rides what appears to be a death train with many elderly passengers. The film is as visually striking as *Daylight* and is filled with a wealth of symbols, which accompany the young man on his quest to find what he has been missing in his life.

Not only was *Nirvana* awarded the prestigious Short Film Award at the International Short Film Festival Oberhausen (which primarily caters to live-action films), but it was also shown on Estonian Television, prior to a speech by the Estonian Prime Minister.

The synopsis of Laas's latest film, *Generatio* (2005), sounds straightforward: "An architect tries to help his wife as she gives birth to their child. As he does he slips into a fantastic journey and experiences all manner of wondrous things between the stars and the sea." As you might expect from the Estonians, things aren't exactly as simple as they appear to be.

Generatio is actually a complex, visually dazzling allegory about history, culture, freedom and the cycles of life. While Laas's use of mixed-media techniques is somewhat new and refreshing for the Estonian animation landscape, his philosophical and ecological concerns point to the past and follow in the footsteps of his predecessors, notably Estonian animators Heino Pars and Mati Kütt.

Generatio was made for a German-produced feature film called *Lost and Found*. Laas was one of six Eastern European filmmakers invited to contribute to the film. "I was invited to a meeting with Nikolaj Nikitin, who is the delegate from Berlinale (the one of the biggest film festivals in Europe)," says Laas. "At the meeting he asked me if I would be interested in joining the project and doing the animation part of the feature."

Laas was excited by the request and jumped at the opportunity. "It was really surprising for me," says Laas, "that feature film makers were interested in having animation in their world!" Laas was given some guidelines for the project — it had to deal with problems between generations in new societies — but beyond that he was given almost total creative freedom. "The producers and other filmmakers have trusted me," adds Laas, "and I had the possibility to do basically what I had written in my script."

From the beginning, Laas wanted to use a mix of animation techniques in *Generatio*. "The idea," says Laas, "was to have all the techniques in the film because they also represent the different generations. Also, because *Generatio* was split up in short segments for *Lost and Found*, so I felt that it would be smoother technically if I used different styles. Different techniques will build different atmospheres for the viewer. The main idea, though, was to show that even beneath these different forms or clothes, the line in life is the same. I think it's important that we recognize and respect how important that is."

While issues of tradition and history lie at the core of *Generatio*, Laas also addresses complex philosophical and ecological themes. For example, water plays an essential part of the film. We are made of water; we rely on water to survive; many philosophers have also suggested that water is the key to harmony in life, that our search for our own rhythm and flow in life is deeply connected with the flow of the rivers. "This ecological viewpoint is very important issue as the continuity of the most important values — the life in the earth," says Laas.

On yet another level, Laas also explores the relations between masculinity and femininity, creation and destruction, and our desire to bring these cycles of life into harmony. *Generatio* is filled with a variety of odd characters (men, bees, a cat, matchstick men, a fetus, and a naked woman) that seem completely disconnected; yet in truth they are all connected, all part of the same stream of life. What interests Laas is uncovering this mysterious essence that unites and separates us all. "Nobody knows, for example, exactly about the soul of the bees and how they know to act collectively, it is not pure ratio, nor is it entirely biological, it is something in between and it is mysterious — that is that."

What is even more intriguing about *Generatio* is how Laas's vision and approach speaks to both the future and past of Estonian animation. Laas's refusal to abide by a singular style is far removed from the recognizable style of, for example, Priit Pärn or Riho Unt, and shows a willingness to explore new technologies. However, Laas's interest in philosophical and ecological issues links him to earlier generations of Estonian animation, particularly Mati Kütt (*Underground, Button's Odyssey*) and Heino Pars (*Songs to the Spring, River of Life*). The clothes might be different, but the essence of life remains the same.

Finding answers is not Laas's primary goal as an artist: he is more interested in stimulating his audience. "For me it is actually very important to activate the viewer — to inspire them to feel or think or follow something on their own. Sometimes art makes people very passive, but sometimes active dreams or visions can follow us through life — even when we will never find the dreambook that will explain it in logical way through words."

Engaging viewers has not been an easy task for Laas. His films are complex and somewhat abstract, and audiences — especially in Estonia — have struggled to embrace his films. "I don't try to make esoteric films," says Laas. "For me, they are quite clear. I don't like to destroy things. I think it's more interesting to unite. Everything has a connection with something else. I like people to talk and communicate so that we are not alone or separated. This is my basic aim."

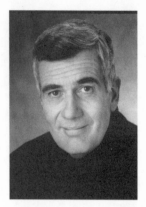

Figure 19.1   John Canemaker

Figure 19.2   *Bottom's Dream*

Figure 19.3   *The Moon and The Son*

CHAPTER 19

John Canemaker
Confessions of an Animator

1956. Elmira, New York. The Cannizzaros had had another argument. Eager to get out of the house, John Cannizzaro Sr. grabbed his boys John Jr. and Tony and took them to see a re-release of the Disney film *Fantasia*. The experience would change 13-year-old John's life:

"In the theatre Dad promptly fell asleep and brother Tony was bored, but I was fascinated by what I saw on the screen. It was literally another world — a controlled, beautifully ordered and colorful world beyond human turmoil — a world I wanted to enter. A fantasy of dancing flowers, flying horses, centaurs, fairies, balletic hippos and alligators, wonderful dinosaurs and the devil himself — and Mickey Mouse! And all moving perfectly to classical music that was new to my ears."

The excited young boy raced to the local library in search of books about *Fantasia*. He found a few, signed them out and went home and made his own drawings. Canemaker (John took this surname because of his father's legal troubles) then learned that a nearby art shop owner had an original cel and background from the *The Sorcerer's Apprentice* episode from *Fantasia*. "He allowed me to take [the cel] home to study. I painted my own version of it. I remember adding special binding liquid to the paint to help adhere it to the celluloid on which I drew Mickey Mouse. It wasn't actually celluloid acetate, but washed-off x-ray sheets from a hospital. So my first cels were blue tinted. Such were the conditions of animation study in upstate New York, circa late 1950s!"

That young boy grew up to be one of the world's foremost animation experts, animation's renaissance man: a noted author of several important books on animation (*Felix* and *Winsor McCay*), historian, teacher and an Oscar-winning animator (*The Moon and The Son*).

Canemaker had been drawing before he saw *Fantasia*. "I always drew from my earliest years, and my parents were proud of my drawing ability, often trotting me out to sketch cartoons for visitors to our home. They paid for a few watercolor lessons with a local artist. But the problem was no one in my family ever went to college, so I had no inclination to do so or any understanding of how to take my natural talent for drawing and interest in the arts to a higher level."

During high school, Canemaker continue to absorb everything he could about animation and even made an animation film called *Animation, Its History and Usages* in 1959. "It was a steal from the Nov. 11, 1955 Disneyland TV program *The Story of the Animated Drawing*. A local teacher with a single-frame Bolex camera shot it with me. It was an ambitious live-action documentary with animation."

With post-secondary animation schools years away, Canemaker had no idea how to get into the animation industry. Instead, he headed to New York to the American Academy of Dramatic Arts.

"I had participated in amateur theatrics locally in Elmira, so I figured I'd fool the public at large and become an actor. (Desperate times, desperate measures.)" In 1961, with $60 in his pocket, 18-year-old Canemaker headed to the Big Apple.

Canemaker's drama studies only lasted a year (he left after he learned that students were not permitted to find professional work), but he remained in New York for the next few years, continuing his acting studies in Greenwich Village (where he was a classmate of young Liza Minnelli) performed off-Broadway and began acting in TV commercials. Canemaker's burgeoning acting career came to a sudden halt in March 1967 when the US army came calling for troops to go to Vietnam.

After serving in the US army for two years, Canemaker returned to New York and his acting career. Using the money he earned from commercials and TV, Canemaker decided to go to college. "I was looking for something else beyond the actor's life, but didn't know what. I knew I was uneducated, so I decided to go to college.

Pursuing a BFA in Communication at Marymount Manhattan College (1971–4) changed my life."

Animation suddenly appeared in Canemaker's life again: in 1973, a teacher gave Canemaker an opportunity to write a paper on the history of Disney animation. A Walt Disney archive had just been opened in Burbank and Canemaker was given the opportunity to go there to research his paper. "What a great opportunity that was! I flew to California, met most of the Nine Old Men (eventually becoming friends with four of them — Frank Thomas, Ollie Johnston, Marc Davis and Ward Kimball), viewed early films, and (best of all) flipped original animation scenes, such as the mushroom dance from *Fantasia*."

After finishing his paper, Canemaker embarked on a career as an animation historian. "Within two years I was animation editor at *Millimeter* magazine and had my first book contract, for *The Animated Raggedy Ann & Andy*."

Meanwhile, Canemaker got his master's degree from New York University (NYU), made a documentary (*Remembering Winsor McCay*) and also wrote and hosted a 1975 CBS documentary on Warner Bros. animation (*The Boys From Termite Terrace*). "By the mid-1970s, I was launched as an animation historian and writer, as well as a journeyman animator."

In 1981, Canemaker was approached by George Roy Hill to animate sequences for his feature film *The World According to Garp* (1982). Canemaker then set up his own studio and the work flowed; during the next thirty years, John Canemaker Productions has designed and directed an array of commissioned works for an impressive list of clients including Derek Lamb, Michael Sporn and Yoko Ono. Canemaker also did work for *Sesame Street*, *The Electric Company*, *Pee-Wee's Playhouse* and, more recently, *The Wonder Pets!* Canemaker also created animation for two award-winning documentaries: *You Don't Have to Die* (1988), about children dealing with cancer, which won HBO an Oscar for Best Documentary Short; and *Break the Silence: Kids Against Child Abuse* (1994), a CBS documentary that won a Peabody Award.

If Canemaker's story stopped here, it would already be pretty damn impressive, but we haven't even gotten to his personal animation films. As an animator Canemaker has created an impressive body of award-winning work.

Canemaker made three animation films in 1974, but his first notable film was *Confessions of a Stardreamer* (1978). Appropriately, *Stardreamer* deals with acting; Canemaker employs wonderful diverse, imaginative and playful animation while an actress friend discusses the ups and downs of her acting pursuits.

"This was my breakthrough film, which garnered wide attention and screenings. The extemporaneous recorded musings of an actress friend of mine about her career provides the springboard for an imaginative fantasy on the fragility of fame." *Confessions* would be the first of Canemaker's films to explore the theme of performance.

The Wizard's Son (1981) follows a more conventional path: modeled on old Disney cartoons, *Wizard's Son* explores, without dialogue, the relationship between a father and son. A smug and demanding wizard wants his young son to follow in his footsteps, but the son has other dreams.

Wizard's Son is an enjoyable film, but has a number of shortcomings: the characters are simply not that interesting and the animation lacks the polish of the old cartoons Canemaker hoped to emulate. "The film doesn't really work, but it was a valuable experiment for me. I felt I needed to learn about story structure and characterization through pantomime. The story is told through personality animation. I became fully aware of my limitations and possibilities as an animation filmmaker." The film also hints at the difficult father/son relationship Canemaker would explore in his finest film, *The Moon and The Son*.

One of animation's essential viewings, *Bottom's Dream* (1983), finds Canemaker in a freewheeling stream-of-consciousness mood. The result is a frenetic dream/trip full of beautiful, potent imagery and breathtaking animation. Inspired by Shakespeare and accompanied by Mendelssohn's *A Midnight Summer's Dream*, *Bottom's Dream* could easily be an outtake from Canemaker's beloved *Fantasia*. "I've always loved Mendelssohn's *Scherzo from A Midnight Summer's Dream* and Shakespeare's magical play, so I made this free-form short in a variety of techniques and styles. After the constriction of *The Wizard's Son* it was a release for me, a film full of fun and playfulness in spirit and method."

Following *Confessions of a Stand-Up* (1993), an expressionist piece about a comedian in the vein of *Confessions of a Stardreamer*, Canemaker returned with the beautiful, subdued lyrical work, *Bridgehampton* (1998); Fred Hersch's gentle Vince Guaraldi-like piano piece is a gentle breeze, a quiet passionate travel mate guiding us through the lush landscapes.

Bridgehampton was inspired by Canemaker's relocation to the Hamptons on Long Island in the late 1980s. "The nearness to nature (flowers, trees, ocean) sparked an intense period of painting, mostly using gouache and watercolor. Which in turn led to a storyboard based on the paintings and eventually this painterly study of the seasons. It was a wonderful 'improvisational' and jazzy collaboration."

In 2004, Canemaker made *The Moon and the Son: An Imagined Conversation* (2004). He calls it "the film I was always meant to make." An extraordinary exploration of Canemaker's difficult relationship with his father, *The Moon and The Son* is a perfect example of how personal, powerful and mature an art form animation can be when it's given the opportunity.

The film is rich with layers of meaning and stories: *The Moon and The Son* is a memoir, fantasy, biography and also a document of the immigration experience of Italians. "I figured I had made many films about other people's lives and concerns, and I had thought about the subject matter for many years; indeed, it affected my life profoundly. I made the film to resolve long-standing emotional issues I still have with my late father. A catharsis in animation. I wanted to find answers to our difficult relationship, to understand the reasons he was always a feared figure in my childhood, why he was always angry and defensive, verbally and physically abusive, and often in trouble with the law."

Canemaker interviewed his father just before his death in 1995 and was surprised by what he learned. "I discovered he was a man of many contradictions — American-born but raised in poverty in Calabria, Italy; a pious Catholic with long ties to organized crime; a twice-decorated World War II hero subsequently convicted of arson; an eager, aggressive go-getter unable to achieve his dreams; a devoted husband and father whose rage and self-inflicted misfortune devastated his family."

Thanks to a residency grant from the Rockefeller Foundation, work on *The Moon and The Son* began in Italy in August 1999. "My studio overlooked Lake Como and each day I made many sketches and conferred with other residents (poets, musicians, writers, artists, academics) about my project (and theirs). It was a great experience — have an entire month to work only on the story for my film, to be surrounded by other artists who encouraged your work, and to be fed and treated so well in such a beautiful setting."

Once the script and storyboard were complete, Canemaker and producer Peggy Stern recorded actor Eli Wallach as the father, and

Canemaker voiced the son. "I remember tearing up at the sound of Eli's voice with an Italian accent behind the microphone. He sounded just like my father. My reading (playing myself) stayed on the track for a long time, but Peg and I finally agreed I was too close to the real events and wasn't able or willing to hit the necessary emotional peaks."

With the help of Wallach, Canemaker and Stern managed to sway John Turturro to come onboard and play the son. "Turturro was interested but very busy. Finally, our patience and persistence paid off and we got him into a recording studio and he did an excellent job.

The final 28-minute short was an instant success. *The Moon and The Son* played in festivals around the world and in March 2006, the film won the Academy Award for Best Animation Short. A few months later, Canemaker won an Emmy for "outstanding graphic and artistic design."

Canemaker admits that the Oscar win was both surprising and satisfying. Despite his body of work as an animator, Canemaker often felt that his film achievements were overshadowed by his career as an historian and teacher. The Oscar win changed people's perceptions of Canemaker: he was now finally recognized and accepted as a great artist. "Present and future assessments of my career must include my filmmaking on an equal footing with my other activities, and that is gratifying."

Still, don't expect Canemaker's life to change with all this fame and praise:

After the Academy Award ceremony and the Governor's Ball, our limo was approaching the Vanity Fair party with the windows down. A fan approached the car and seeing my Oscar in hand, he said "Whad'ja win for?" "Animation," says I. "Oh," said the young man, "can I have your autograph?" "Sure." I began signing his scrap of paper when he looked quizzical and asked, "You're Nick Park, aren't you?" "No," I said as he grabbed his paper back and disappeared into the crowd! (Keeps ya humble.)

These days, Canemaker remains extremely busy: aside from his teaching at NYU, he has finished a documentary with Peggy Stern called *Chuck Jones: Memories of Childhood* (2008); his latest book *Two Guys Named Joe: Master Animation Storytellers Joe Grant and Joe Ranft* was published in late 2009; and he's also started preparing a new personal film.

To call Canemaker's achievements in animation "impressive" is an understatement: his writing work alone has filled a massive gap in animation history. Canemaker's writing has unearthed many forgotten and unsung voices from animation's past: men and women whose accomplishments were too frequently brushed aside by the cold shrug of time.

Canemaker's films reflect that same empathetic quality. His films have often dealt with complex characters (including his own father), but Canemaker never throws them under the bus. Instead, Canemaker tries desperately to understand their difficulties and motivations so that we may see their humanity.

John Canemaker is everything that is right about the world of animation: a humble, caring, generous man with a deep love and passion for an art form that it too frequently labelled as facile entertainment.

"I have led a charmed life and know how fortunate I have been to meet these great artists and pass on information about their art and lives through my articles, documentary films and books. Today is an exciting time to be an animator and the future is wide open for personal, independent visions."

Figure 20.1   Joanna Quinn

Figure 20.2   Beryl and Vince

Figure 20.3   *Dreams and Desires: Family Tie*

CHAPTER 20

Joanna Quinn

Beryl, *Britannia* and Bum-Wiping Bears

I'd venture to guess that anyone who owns a television has seen the work of English animator Joanna Quinn. I'm not talking about her extraordinary short films, *Girls Night Out*, *Body Beautiful* and *Dreams and Desires: Family Ties*, but her memorable commercials for Charmin toilet paper featuring some big cuddly bears that like to maintain personal hygiene after taking a personal moment in the woods. Of course, most viewers have no idea they're watching the work of one of the world's most successful and acclaimed animators.

Visually, the Charmin commercials bear the undeniable stamp of Joanna Quinn, but that's where the similarities fade. There's nothing precious or feminine about Joanna Quinn's animation films: they are aggressive, edgy, provocative, saucy and funny as hell.

To find the roots of Quinn's artistic traits, just take a gander at her childhood:

"I was a tomboy and a bit feral. All my friends were boys and I loved climbing, fighting and not washing."

At age five, Quinn was a mascot for a local teenage gang that took her to fights for good luck. Age six was a particularly exciting year for Quinn. She made money by tying a rope across the pavement and made old ladies pay her to be allowed to pass. The money likely paid for her smoking habit — every Saturday morning she'd inhale about ten cigarettes with a friend. As if that wasn't enough, Quinn was kidnapped by two nuns. They took her to church and made her pray for redemption. Police eventually found her the same day.

The one normal trait of Quinn's childhood was her love of drawing. Her passion was so strong that her bedroom walls were covered with drawings. In fact, Quinn wanted to draw so much that she momentarily dreamed of going to prison because she "liked the idea of being left alone to draw."

During this early stage, Quinn also accepted the fleeting nature of drawings. "I remember vividly when I was about six my mom bought me a freestanding blackboard and chalks and I did a fantastic drawing of our Ford Anglia car. I did observational drawings even then! Then I realized that I had to wipe it off if I wanted to do any more drawing. I think from this point on I stopped being precious about my drawings and would be happy to spend hours doing a drawing and as long as I was able to show everybody after I had finished, then I was happy to rub it out and start again."

Her first published illustration was in a gay magazine. "I was about 12. The drawing was of a vicar and a choirboy." Her grandmother had a copy of the drawing framed on her wall.

A couple of years later, Quinn tried to get a job with the Beano comic but was told to finish school and go to art college first. She eventually did get her first art job at age 16, doing illustrations for a magic shop's catalogue. "Davenports Magic shop was a famous old shop opposite the British Museum. I did diagrams of how to do the tricks."

After high school, Quinn took a foundation art course at Goldsmiths College in London followed by a three-year graphics course at Middlesex University.

Animation entered Quinn's world for good during an animation class in 1984. The students were given an animation assignment, and rather than go to the library and read up a bit on animation, the stubborn Quinn decided to figure animation out for herself. The result was her first film, *Superdog*. "When I filmed the walking legs on the video line tester and played it back I was dumbstruck — it worked! It was the same excitement I felt when I developed my first photograph except even better. I suddenly felt a sense of great creative power — imagine being able to make things move! I still get that feeling but less frequently and often with other people's animation!"

Quinn now knew that she wanted to be an animator, even if she wasn't quite sure how one made a living making animation. "I didn't really think of it as a possible profession as I didn't really know any animators or how you could earn money from it." It wasn't until after Quinn made her graduation film, *Girls Night Out* (1989) that she began to realize that maybe she could make a living doing animation.

In *Girls Night Out*, a group of female factory workers head out to a strip club to celebrate their colleague, Beryl's birthday. Beryl is clearly excited about the evening. She has a dull job and an even duller husband. During her night out, Beryl unleashes her passion and desires. The women hoot and holler at the male stripper (a nice inversion of the usual gender types). Quinn's drawings are rough, almost punkish. The women and their environment are rather dour and average; the women have bad hair, flab and too much makeup. They're normal, everyday women — not big boobed, curvy caricatures. *Girls Night Out* is an unharnessed celebration of female desire.

"During my college years I became quite politically active and learnt about feminism. It was this that inspired me to choose an older, 'ordinary' woman as the unlikely central character in my first really personal film. It was identification with the underdog, the exploited or the politically unrepresented."

Girls Night Out also marked the debut of Quinn's alter ego, Beryl. "Because I was, in the main, brought up by a single parent — my mother — in quite difficult circumstances, it's likely that I used her as a model — someone struggling but uncomplaining, battling against adversity to provide stability and security. It was a combination of all these influences then which undoubtedly provoked the 'genesis of Beryl.'"

Using completion grants she received from Channel 4 and S4C (a Welsh television channel), Quinn completed the film six months after she left college. *Girls Night Out* did extremely well at festivals and many people watched it when it aired on Channel 4. Suddenly, Quinn was offered money to make a second film. "That was when I realized I could make a living doing animation and felt justified in putting 'animator' on my business card."

Beryl returned as the star in Quinn's second film, *Body Beautiful* (1990). A Japanese company has taken over the factory where Beryl works. Beryl has bigger problems though, in particular, a brash, smug macho prick named Vince. Vince continually mocks Beryl's weight in front of the other workers. Fed up, Beryl signs up for the company's bodybuilding competition so she can show up Vince and feel better about herself. Quinn's animation and character design is again edgy, frantic and full of life. However, the story feels a bit less organic than *Girls Night Out*. Perhaps this problem stems from trying to tackle too many issues at once.

Aside from the theme of the female underdog and Beryl's ongoing struggles as a middle-aged woman, *Body Beautiful* also dives into larger political commentary. "With the American experience in Vietnam, the liberation movements in Angola and Mozambique, and the Sandinista's experience in Nicaragua still fresh in our minds. We thought of making Beryl's fight a metaphor for these struggles," says Quinn's partner, Les Mills, who has scripted all of their films.

During the time of production, Wales had also become a popular target for Japanese investment. "The biggest of these were Sony's TV factory at Bridgend and the Panasonic complex in Cardiff," says Mills. "We decided to reflect this by updating Beryl's work situation from a cake factory to one of these factories, specifically the Sony one."

In 1991, Quinn was approached by French producer Didier Brunner to participate in a series called *Cabaret*, comprised of films based on works by Toulouse-Lautrec and made by different animation directors.

"Initially," says Quinn, "I said I couldn't do it because it looked like I would be working on *Famous Fred* [a 1998 TV special], but then *Fred* was delayed so it turned out I did have time. However by the time I agreed I had lost a few months of production time, so I proposed to Didier that it had more of a sketchbook quality to the animation, with less color and limited backgrounds."

Quinn settled on Lautrec's painting of two women lying on a bed together. "I liked the idea of challenging the artist's portrayal of these women as prostitutes, as if we are a voyeur peeking into their sordid world; a world in which the artist seems to have an intimate relationship with the women who allow him to paint them relaxing on a bed together, hinting at their lesbian relationship. I wanted to depict them as ordinary 'working women' who were posing as models for the artist in return for money."

This is precisely what Quinn achieved in *Elles*. The sketchbook approach adds another layer of voyeurism to the film. The viewer is watching the artist's interpretation of the two women and, in a sense, also observing the artist via her sketchbook. Under Quinn's confident hand, the women also quickly resemble women from Beryl's world: plump, funny, raunchy and freewheeling.

Achieving her ideas was a challenge because Quinn was asked to work with a French scriptwriter, Hortense Guillemard. Quinn quickly discovered that they had very different attitudes towards the women in the painting. "Hortense was very French and wanted to celebrate the sexuality of the two women and make it more into a romp. To me that was an anathema as I thought it was reinforcing the exploitation of these women by the artist but I gave in!"

Quinn lost the battle, but maintains that she thoroughly enjoyed the experience. "It's not something I would ever have done if I had been working on my own. That's why I enjoy working with other people so much, because you are forced to see things from another perspective and your own beliefs are challenged and enriched."

Elles also marked a turning point in terms of Quinn's approach to animation. With only three months to make the film, Quinn was forced to work much more quickly than she was accustomed to. Locked away in her house in Spain, Quinn frantically worked on the film. Because she didn't have a line tester with her in Spain, Quinn had to act out all of the film's movements and actions before she started animating.

"I observed the movement over and over again and made quick thumbnail sketches of all the key positions. I copied those keys directly onto my animation paper and ploughed through the film. When I got back to my line tester in the UK I tested all my animation, to my surprise and joy, all the movement worked and I didn't have to redo anything! This was an enormous lesson I learnt about the importance of observation."

With *Britannia* (1993), Quinn leaves Beryl behind and goes for the direct political attack. Based on a book by Madge Dresser, *Britannia* is a short, snippy summation of the history of Britain through the eyes of a bulldog. Directed by an unseen female voice, the bulldog embarks on a legacy of imperialism, slavery, violence and cultural appropriation (tea is an example). As the dog continues to stump on the world, the voice becomes increasingly deranged and menacing. Finally, the world outgrows the bulldog. The bulldog, now forgotten and impotent, transforms into a harmless little poodle — nothing more than a lap dog.

Britannia took a long two years to make. "The first year," says Quinn was spent getting the storyboard right. After initial close consultation with the producer I was given quite a lot of freedom to come up with the storyboard. Condensing this vast subject matter down to 5 minutes was an enormous task and at times I thought it was going to be impossible and found myself struggling." To help make the storyboard more clear and concise, Quinn and her producer brought on a left-wing newspaper cartoonist, Steve Bell, to help finish the film.

In 1996, Quinn was invited to direct one of Geoffrey Chaucer's *Canterbury Tales*, which was being commissioned by S4C for the BBC and HBO. Because of the strong female characters in the story, Quinn opted for *The Wife of Bath's Tale*.

A knight rapes a woman; he is captured and presented before the Queen. The Queen gives him 12 months to find out what a woman most desires or else he will be put to death. The knight races off and knocks at every door, but receives conflicting answers from the many men he asks. Upon his return, the knight meets an ugly old hag in the woods. She agrees to tell him the answer if he promises to do anything she asks of him. He agrees and the Queen spares his life. Freed, the knight suddenly learns that he must wed the ugly old hag. When he agrees to give all power in the marriage to her, she turns into a young, sexy hottie, and love and other such saucy things blossom.

Wife of Bath is Quinn's weakest film. Her animation is typically remarkable, rich and detailed, but the story feels too rushed, too superficial. Quinn, fortunately, doesn't argue with this assessment. "This was a very challenging film to make because I had imagined I would have complete control over the film. However I very soon realized that the script editor of the whole series had ultimate control. When I look at this film now, I really enjoy the quality of the drawing and the animation but feel disappointed with the storytelling and most of the voices."

Given Quinn's remarkable success as an independent and commissioned animator, it's stunning to realize that there is a 16-year gap between *Body Beautiful* and *Dreams and Desires: Family Ties* (2006). "Because of the long gap," says Mills, "both of us were literally gasping to produce another personal and original film. Clare Kitson was still the commissioning editor for Channel 4 UK. At this time there was a 10-minute slot after the Channel 4 evening news which had been showing short animated films at this time five days of the week. Clare hinted that a series of inter-related Beryl shorts could fit into those slots perfectly." Taking the hint, Mills and Quinn began working on a script that would use a video diary as a structural device to link the five segments.

The basic idea was that we would see an ageing, tired Beryl attempting to revive the passions of her youth. "The video diary idea," adds Mills, "seemed to be the perfect vehicle to structure Beryl's new life, to communicate her feelings, to foster her newfound ambitions, and ultimately, to fulfill her dreams and desires."

Inspired by the gift of a video camera from her sister, Beryl begins absorbing film history and then films the wedding of a friend. The result is a madcap journey through the absurdities of a wedding that finds Beryl interrupting the wedding by using an old man and his wheelchair to take a tracking shot, and getting sloshed and strapping the camera atop a dog (Digger, a reference to the Russian avant-garde filmmaker Dziga Vertov). Through the dog's eyes, we stumble upon a threesome that appears to involve the groom but not the wife. After her disastrous (depending on the perspective of course) cinematic debut, Beryl sits alone on her bed on the phone conveying her frustrations to her sister. Her solemn mood soon gives way to new dreams and desires; Beryl keeps moving, keeps hoping.

"The idea of taking a diary format and using it in animation to directly talk to an audience seemed to be a fairly unique concept (at that time)," says Mills. "It gave great scope to break many conventions, to confront audiences, to make reference to documentary formats and traditions, to get incredibly intimate with the central character and above all to carry the narrative forward in a highly structured if somewhat predictable way."

In an ideal world Quinn would, like all indie animators, be able to work solely on personal projects, but the world, of course, is far from ideal. Strangely, while animation has become more visible and popular than ever, animators are also seeing fewer funding opportunities. England is one of the supreme examples. "When I left college in the late eighties it was relatively easy to get money for short animation," says Quinn. "Channel 4 was new and looking to invest in independent producers. When Clare Kitson arrived at the Channel then the whole British animation era began. Single-handedly she nurtured a whole generation of young filmmakers, and British animation soon became seen as challenging and groundbreaking. Today the situation is very different. Channel 4 has no animation department and S4C animation department has been consumed into children's entertainment."

Quinn is comfortable making short films and commercials and sees no reason to change at the moment. Oddly enough, Quinn's biggest successes have come on the commercial side. When *Famous Fred* (1998), the TV special she directed, received an Oscar nomination, Quinn received offers to do commercial work. Her commercials for Charmin toilet paper and Whiskas cat food have in turn funded personal films like *Dreams and Desires*.

Currently Quinn is at work on the next *Dreams and Desires*

episode tentatively called *Affairs of the Art*. "We get involved with Beryl's childhood and family — growing up with her sister Beverly, and Beryl's own kids — Colin and Julie," says Quinn."

Joanna Quinn's reign as an internationally respected animator stems not just from her talent, but also from her openness, optimism and perseverance. "I'm always being stretched, pushed and challenged, and made to do things that perhaps I sometimes find a little uncomfortable. But then once I'm drawing and getting results, it's really exciting — in fact it's when I'm happiest."